The KNOM/ Father Jim Poole Story

God bless you!
Fr. Jim

by Louis L. Renner, S.J.

Binford & Mort Publishing
Portland, Oregon

THE KNOM/FATHER JIM POOLE STORY

Manufactured in the United States of America.

Library of Congress Catalog Card Number: 85-71950
ISBN: 0-8323-0444-1 (softcover)

First Edition 1985

This book is dedicated in loving memory
to the following departed members
of the KNOM family:

Marty Clarke

Harry Gallagher

Diana Gardenier

John Huck

Dennis Pikongonna

Luella Poole

Dephane Sporrer

May they rest in God's peace.

WITHOUT WHOSE ASSISTANCE
THIS BOOK
COULD NOT HAVE BEEN PUBLISHED

Charles and Matilda Akers
Joanne Ambrosi
Mr. & Mrs. Robert C. Anderson
Raymond Atchak
Mathew and Marlene Back
Don Banas
Sister Victoria Bartley
Anthony J. Brake
Frances M. Bretholl
Helen Burke
Margie Cain
Juanita Diaz Camilon
Matthew P. and Mary Campion
Frances Cassidy
Catholic Daughters of America,
  No. 2003
George Cebula II
George Chauvin
In Memory of Marty Clarke
Tim Cochran
Thomas J. Coleman
Ann M. Corrigan
M. Cosko
Marie Costello
Albert Cryan
Mary D'Ambrosia
Ray W. Dahm
Elsie Darnell
Hurbert and Miriam Dennis
Mary Herzog Diebel
Mr. & Mrs. Bob Dieringer
Marie Dieringer
William and Elizabeth Drowns
Jack Dudley
Fr. Fallert
Miles and Henrietta Flood
Helen and Everett Ford
Leonard and Florence Gay
Patricia Gerrard
Bishop Francis D. Gleeson, S.J.
Susanne Grogan
Rayna Hamm

Mike Hansen
Honoroa R. Hauswirth
Helyne Holliday
Holy Family Parish, Yakima
Bishop Michael J. Kaniecki, S.J.
Mrs. Fred Keiser
Teresa Kosiba
Mr. & Mrs. Jim Lee
Marie Logan
Rev. Paul B. Macke, S.J.
Ann Kevin Mawn
Most Rev. J. J. McEleney
Yvonne E. McHugh
Catherine Miller
Mission Circle 123, Alhambra, CA
Thomas J. Mullin
John and Julie Noble
Harry Owens, Jr.
Msgr. Peter J. Owens
Cynthia Pendleton
Melvin and Hazel Peters
Dr. and Mrs. Robert C. Poole
Capt. Michael J. Renner
William and Bernice Renner
Richard and Mary Santi
Nick and Robyn Scales
Carolyn Schubert
Dorothy Shea
Mary E. Stone
Mr. & Mrs. Jim Tighe
Joseph and Leona Tucker
Jackie and Peter Van Nort
Jack and Julia Weber
Bishop Robert L. Whelan, S.J.
Thomas White
Anita Williams
Joseph W. Witmer
Elizabeth C. Witt
Henry Wolak
Pauline Yett
Thomas M. Zabresky

TABLE OF CONTENTS

Transmission 1

Boyhood and Youth: 1923-41

The KNOM/Father Jim Poole story began in Cle Elum, Washington, where on 18 May 1923 James Elwood Poole was born to Chester R. Poole and Luella Burke Poole. His brother Robert — now Dr. Robert C. Poole — preceded him by two years; his sister Helen — now Mrs. Everett F. Ford — followed him by three.

When Jim was four years old, the family moved from Cle Elum — where his dad had run a silent movie theatre — to Klamath Falls, Oregon. After two years there, they moved again, to Redding, California. There Jim completed the third, fourth, and fifth grades. His dad worked in stores both in Klamath Falls and Redding.

Helen's early memories of Jim are that he was always kind to everyone, that he willingly played her imaginary games with her, that he loved animals. The family had rabbits, and whenever one died, Jim would put the body in a metal box — along with rose petals — seal the box with wax, and bury the bunny with solemn ceremony. He and his pet dog, Pat, regularly slept side by side in the same bed, under the same covers, Pat's head on the pillow right next to Jim's.

"All was happy up to the fifth grade," recalls Father Jim painfully, "then social life made it clear dad was an alcoholic and all went to hell." Taking the three children — and the ten dollars left in her purse — Mrs. Poole boarded the train and went north to live with her parents in Tacoma, Washington.

There Jim was enrolled in St. Patrick's Grade School run by the Dominican Sisters. Fifty years later his seventh grade teacher, Sister M. Amelia, remembered him as an average student, an altar boy, a very ambitious lad who never gave her any trouble.

During his last years in grade school, Jim had an altar built in his bedroom. According to Helen, he was serious about religion and always had a very deep devotion to the Blessed Virgin Mary. "Now I don't want you to think," she hastened to add, "that he was a quiet little stay-at-home, hands-folded-in-prayer type of person. Anything but! He always loved and lived life to the fullest."

Jim did not engage in sports; instead he spent his after-school hours and weekends in scouting activities and working to earn spending money and money for the struggling family. "My brother Bob and I," he remembered many years later, "were working to pay bills and buy beef heart, and hamburger meat at ten cents a pound. Ours were the only incomes." Grocery store owner W. E. "Fritz" Gosselin — whom Father Jim honors as his second father — was his scoutmaster and employer. Fritz found Jim a very capable scout leader and a hard worker in his store, as well as a reliable caretaker of his yard.

In 1937 Jim entered Bellarmine, a prep school in Tacoma run by the Jesuits. The self-confidence that has characterized the whole of his adult life manifested itself strikingly already during his high school years. Classmate Paul W. Greiwe remembered him as "a handsome individual who knew who he was and where he was going."

As Prefect of Our Lady's Sodality at Bellarmine, Jim displayed his singular talent for fundraising when he motivated his fellow sodalists to raise enough money to buy a large statue of the Virgin Mary to be erected on the school campus. His boyhood piety and devotion to Mary continued on through his high school years — but it surely did not cramp his style, his zest for enjoying life. Helen wrote of him, "I don't think he ever missed a dance or a new movie that came to town — or near town." However, she — and all the girls at the girls' academy — used to think it strange that he never asked the same girl out twice.

Neill R. Meany — co-editor with Jim of the *Bellarmine Lion*, the school paper, and now his fellow Jesuit priest — recalled how Jim as a high schooler "was a P.R. man and a leader from the word 'go,'" and how he staged very imaginative, large-scale displays to boost fund drives in the school. One of these consisted of a hall-long racetrack with little cars pulled along by strings to show the progress and relative positions of the various competing classes.

Neill recalled, too, how Jim chose most colorful, dramatic themes for school dances and assemblies. A standout was his 1941 "Dictator Dip" featuring Hitler and Mussolini. At one point a siren sounded, and balsa gliders swooped down on the audience from the rafters above. Certain gliders had a mark on the wing. Anyone fortunate enough to catch one of these gliders was entitled to special refreshments at the concessions booth.

Such were Jim's persuasive powers over the school administration that it allowed him to put on a "Quiz Show" in the study hall every Friday afternoon. One class was pitted against another in answering questions on current events, music, sports, and the like. The whole production was staged as if it were taking place in a real radio studio. Jim — who else? — talking into a make-believe microphone, emceed the show, while over in a corner at a fake but real-looking console sat a fellow student, wearing fake earphones, twisting knobs and switching levers.

"Once he set his sights on an idea or an ideal," said Neill of Jim, "he stayed with it, bulldoggedly until it was realized."

Transmission 2
Seminary Days and Ordination to the Priesthood: 1941-1956

"In the eyes of our friends and family," wrote Helen, "Jim was the most unlikely candidate for the priesthood that ever was." Nevertheless, toward the end of his high school years, there was no doubt in his mind that he was being drawn, called mysteriously, unmistakably, irresistibly to the priesthood. On 30 June 1941 he entered the Jesuit novitiate at Sheridan, Oregon.

After a noviceship of two years he took the three simple but perpetual vows of poverty, chastity, and obedience. He was now a "scholastic" — a Jesuit term for its seminarians — and a full-fledged member of the Society of Jesus, and ready to move to the other end of the building for two years of intensive college courses. The emphasis was mostly on the humanities: Latin, Greek, English, History. Drama and oratory were also emphasized. When Shakespeare's *Julius Caesar* was put on, Jim played the role of Antony. His rendition of the famous "Friends, Romans, countrymen..." speech was long remembered.

In 1945 Jim moved on to Mount Saint Michael's on the outskirts of Spokane for three years of philosophical studies. He spent the years 1948-50 at Holy Cross Mission on the Yukon, where he was prefect of the boys. With those two years began his lifelong love affair with Alaska and Alaska's people.

At Holy Cross Jim was truly in his element. The boarding school and he seemed to have been made for one another. It was staffed by Jesuit priests and lay brothers, and Sisters of St. Ann, and was very much alive with several hundred Eskimo and Indian children, to whom Jim was "Fadder Poole."

Holy Cross Mission on the Yukon about as it appeared when "Mr." Poole was there, 1948-1950. The picture was taken in early spring. Ice is still on the river; piles of manure dot the fields. (Alaskan Shepherd *Collection*)

Sister M. George Edmond described life at Holy Cross during the late 1940s as "...rough. Dame Poverty was the mistress of the mission." Of Jim she wrote, "the smiling, gentlemanly scholastic, because of his happy outlook, his generosity with his time and talents, contributed much to the happiness of the children as well as to that of the missionaries."

Sister M. Ida Brasseur, the cook at Holy Cross at the time, said of Jim that "he was always trying to brighten everyone's life." This he did in various ways. For the boys under his care, "his guys," he begged little extras from the cook. He would look for any excuse to initiate a party, a holiday, a picnic. To pass the time, he once related the Kon-Tiki story to the boys and girls traveling on an open barge to a distant berry field. He had a knack for turning the tedious chores of the children into fun and games. In the evening, when they were in bed, he often entertained them with his gift for storytelling.

Ghost stories continued to be his specialty — and the kids loved them. Long before he ever set foot in Alaska, he told ghost stories. While still in grade school, he used to seat his sister Helen and cousins on a darkened stairway and tell them ghost stories.

It was at Holy Cross that Jim first "got the bug" about a real communications network, according to Father Robert Kirsch of the Archdiocese of Santa Fe. Bob and Jim were together at Holy Cross. For both of them the 26th of February, 1950, was a truly memorable day, for on that day Jesuit Brother George J. Feltes got the ham rig KL7EN on the air, and so established — for the first time — direct vocal contact between the Catholic missions of Alaska and the outside world. Jim and Bob had worked closely with Feltes on this radio project, and both, therefore, enjoyed a personal triumph at its success. At this time Holy Cross Mission also had an in-house station, KAJX. Mostly it was Jim who operated it.

In winter, on the nearby slough, the mission also had a

skating rink, dubbed, not surprisingly, "Poole's pool." Jim, according to Bob, was an excellent skater and taught skating to the children. They were often in mute admiration of his dazzling capers on the ice. Jim's Holy Cross years — very happy years for him — came to an end all too quickly. In the fall of 1950 he began theological studies at Alma College, near Los Gatos, California. While at Alma he wrote numerous letters to friends in Alaska, sent literally tons of clothes, candy, equipment north, and maintained a regular ham radio schedule with Holy Cross. In Spokane, on 20 June 1953, he was ordained a priest. He himself described his ordination day as "the greatest day of my life."

Ordination was followed by a fourth year of theology at Alma, and then an additional year of spiritual formation at Port Townsend, Washington. Next, working out of Seattle, Father Jim spent a year in the Pacific Northwest raising funds for the missions of northern Alaska.

Transmission 3
Lower Yukon and St.
Marys Ministries: 1956-64

By 1956 Father Jim was back in Alaska. His first assign-
ment there as a priest was that of pastor of the lower
Yukon Eskimo villages of Mountain Village, Pilot Station,
and Marshall. Of these he made the rounds by outboard,
dogsled, and commercial airplane.

While still a pastor on the Yukon, Father Jim — clearly
a man to the media born — already had visions of an
Alaska-wide Catholic newspaper and of a radio station.
On 1 April 1959, from Marshall, he wrote to his bishop,
Francis D.Gleeson, S.J., "We have been discussing a radio
station. What are your thoughts on the subject?"

Father Jim as pastor of lower Yukon River villages, 1957. *(Oregon Province Archives)*

When in the fall of 1959 the school year at St. Marys Mission on the Andreafsky River began, the mission boarding school had a new man in charge, Father Jim. It is hard to determine which ministry he liked more, that in the villages, or that in the school. He threw himself heart and soul into both. It seems, however, that — being a gregarious man, a big-family man — he preferred the school ministry. His devotion to St. Marys while he served there and his abiding love for it ever after seem to bear this out.

At St. Marys, as at Holy Cross, he was soon a hit with all at the mission, especially with the kids. Brother Robert L. Benish, S.J., of St. Marys recalled how Father Jim liked to spring unexpected holidays, movies, picnics, joyful surprises on the school's staff and its charges. He was, according to Benish, "interested in everybody, most generous, great with the kids, a great storyteller."

While Father Jim was unquestionably a success as a school administrator, he was not — and he will be the first to admit it — made for the classroom, the academic life. He was not an educator in the traditional sense of the word. It was in the media, specifically in radio, that he saw his chief instrument for educating, for getting out the word, the "Good News."

Shortly after arriving at St. Marys, he thought to himself: Instead of addressing just a small congregation on Sunday, why not reach out to the whole village, all week long? Being a man not only of dreams but also of drive, he was soon doing just that — through a public address system wired into all the homes of the village.

This "little-to-the-village radio" — as Father Jim described his network to Bishop Gleeson — proved to be an immediate success. But it raised the further questions — and he kept pestering his bishop with them —: Instead of reaching only 30 homes in one village, why not reach out to the many, many villages scattered far and wide over the tundra, along the shores of the Bering Sea, and along the riverbanks and sloughs of western Alaska? Why not

St. Marys Mission on the Andreafsky River as it appeared circa 1960. (Alaskan Shepherd *Collection*)

bring the good news of Christ, His peace, joy, hope to the thousands of Eskimos and Indians living for the most part in relative isolation and cut off from the mainstream of 20th-century realities, and yet affected — often quite adversely — by outside influences? He felt strongly that those people could be reached through radio, and through radio be given the ultimate help — the help to help themselves come to grips with new ways of life and cultural conflict.

As time passed, the question of a Catholic radio station for western Alaska kept haunting Father Jim ever more and more. It became an obsession with him. He was especially troubled to see how the Arctic Broadcasting Company, the fundamentalist radio station in Nome, KICY, on the air since April 1960, had the whole field to itself, and was having a very noticeable impact on the people of western Alaska. "They outjumped us on this deal," he wrote to Bishop Gleeson on 23 March 1961, "but I don't see why we can't at least catch up with them."

With remarkable boldness he admitted to Bishop Gleeson to being "really quite hot on the subject," and he proposed that a radio station be given top priority in diocesan planning. "Let's get this thing going," he wrote. "It will do great work for all of our missionaries. Sometimes I wonder if we couldn't let everything sit a year and work on this deal, which is very much on the progressive side."

Progressive thought and action were called for at the time Father Jim felt, because "the twentieth century has reached the Alaska bush. Gradually the Native people find themselves forced to adopt modern ways. This is a dramatic change for most, who have lived in a primitive hunting culture, a closed circle, and isolated for their entire lives. Many of these people find themselves lost in this new world. It is called 'culture shock.' "

Father Jim envisioned the proposed station as doing something quite different from simply hard-sell religious programming after the manner of KICY. The whole lives of the people were to be its concern. He was aware that "changing diets and habits with the coming of civilization have created health and sanitation problems on an incredible scale. You find evidence of these difficulties in the hearing loss among one third of the Native people, in the intestinal and respiratory diseases, in the suicide and alcoholism statistics, and in the eyes of the teenagers." He hoped to do something about this — even if only in a limited way — through radio. The radio approach, he was persuaded, had to be down-to-earth, practical, focusing on temporal — economic, social, bodily — needs as much as on spiritual ones.

Although Father Jim's pleas to Bishop Gleeson for the go-ahead with the proposed radio station did not fall on deaf ears, they did fall on nearly empty pockets. However, Bishop Gleeson — persuaded of the worthiness of the cause and that Father Jim could himself raise the funds and round up enough volunteer help to put up and operate a station — did give the project the green light and his blessing. More the bishop could not do. If Father Jim's personal dream of being "a missionary by microphone," as he put it, was meant to become a reality, he himself would, almost single-handedly, have to make it such.

Transmission 4

Portland and Barrow: 1964-66

"I thought the end of the world had come," wrote Father Jim from Portland in the fall of 1964. Quite unexpectedly his years at what he called his "beloved St. Marys" came to an end. He was called south to join the staff of Jesuit High in Portland. He was assigned to teach religion, speech, and Latin. He had also the "not-much-sought-after job"

Father Jim as pastor of St. Patrick's parish, Barrow, 1966. *(Oregon Province Archives)*

of Athletic Director. When time allowed, he went about showing Alaskan films and begging prayers and support for his "latest brain child," a radio station for the bush of western Alaska.

By now radio was so much a part of Father Jim's thinking and dreaming that he referred to himself as "your roving reporter, transmitting from a new frequency." And the loud-and-clear message he was transmitting was that he needed cash — lots of it — and that getting it would not be easy.

With his whole heart still in Alaska, the Portland year was not an easy one for him. "I really get homesick," he wrote, "for the old icebox and the warmhearted people who live in it."

By his own admission, he spent half of his time dreaming about a radio station. But he did more than just dream, pray, and collect money. Thanks to the kindness of a station owner in Portland, he was able to get valuable radio experience. In the space of one week he taped for broadcasting more than 20 short sermons. He also scouted around for volunteer lay helpers, talked with engineers, and, in general, did all he could to learn the ropes of the radio business. And the cash began to trickle in. At the end of his year in exile he had several thousand dollars banked toward the launching of the hoped-for station.

With almost the same abruptness with which Father Jim had found himself in Portland, he next found himself at the top of the world, at Barrow. He arrived there on 24 July 1965. "We are meeting the town and getting to really know and like the people," he wrote several weeks later. The people, both Eskimo and white, he found very friendly. Himself he described as "a pretty happy boy to be back at work in Alaska."

Since his priestly duties took up only part of his workday, he found time to render public service. Six weeks after his arrival in Barrow he began taking an official census of the town. Census-taking was not a new venture for him. In 1950 he served as official census-taker in Holy Cross.

About this same time he learned that the Barrow treasury was so depleted that the policemen could not be paid. He volunteered to collect retail taxes from stores and businesses. "It was really funny," he recalled, "because there were no books to consult. We had to take the word of the businessmen. We were not overly popular."

While in Barrow he also served as a member of the Chamber of Commerce and of the Civic Improvement Board. In addition, he was president of the Barrow Youth Committee, and scoutmaster.

However, in spite of all his commitments, sacred and secular, thoughts of a radio station continued to occupy the forefront of his mind. He still had no definite idea as to what town or village might be the location best suited for it. Early in 1965 Bethel seemed to him a good place for it. While still in Portland he had written to Bishop Gleeson and enumerated the features that recommended Bethel. It was centrally located, surrounded by flat country, was a transportation hub, had a hospital that could help with his planned "medical educational program," had fairly reliable electrical power and mail service.

By the end of the year, however, Father Jim's focus had shifted from Bethel to Nome. Several factors accounted for this. On a visit to Bethel he had learned that the group there that had at one time shown an interest in having a radio station in its community reacted with "Not interested; we have enough church stations already," when it was told that the proposed station would be church owned and operated. Moreover, he was hoping at the time that the Diocese of Fairbanks would buy out KICY. In any case, Nome seemed to be in every respect just as good a site for a station as Bethel.

When Father Jim began the new year 1966 in Barrow, he had no idea how long he would continue on there, nor when he might be allowed to take concrete steps toward the establishment of a radio station. Meanwhile, money for it kept coming in. By the end of January he had about

$6,500 in the radio fund. He was happy with his work in Barrow, but openly admitted that the radio project still took up most of his dreaming time.

More than Father Jim realized, his bishop, too, was dreaming the radio dream; and, to help make it a reality, he reassigned Father Jim — to Nome.

Transmission 5
Pastor of St. Joseph's Parish, Nome: 1966-67

Father Jim moved to Nome in the summer of 1966. This former gold-rush city of some 25,000 was now a town of around 2,400, in large part Eskimo. Water was still bought and delivered by the gallon; the "honey bucket"

Noralee Irvin, KNOM's first support volunteer, 1967. *(KNOM Collection)*

was the sewer system. Electrical power was not very reliable. None of the streets were paved.

From Jesuit High, Father Jim had written to Bishop Gleeson that he thought the running of a radio station a more or less full-time job for a priest. He was now in a position to proceed with the radio project. However, he was now also in charge of the relatively large St. Joseph's parish. This dual responsibility presented him with a formidable challenge. He embraced it with enthusiasm.

On 7 July 1966 Father Jim informed Bishop Gleeson that he had joined the Nome Chamber of Commerce and the Rotary Club. He also told the bishop that merely examining a list of radio equipment really made him "get into the mood of thinking that we are finally going to get the radio station going and on the air." He estimated that $30,000 would be needed to launch it. By mid-September he had banked a third of this amount.

When he first began thinking about a radio station, Father Jim thought also in terms of lay volunteers to help staff and finance it. The first of his many, many devoted Nome volunteers was a "very willing and generous soul, an old friend from St. Marys," Noralee Irvin. She was with him in Nome almost from the day he arrived there. Noralee, originally from Schenectady, New York, admitted to having "a childhood dream of going to Alaska." From a college classmate she heard about Brother Gerald J. O'Malley, S.J., stationed at St. Marys at the time. The two began corresponding; and, in 1963, after graduating from the College of St. Rose in Albany, New York, Noralee went to St. Marys as a lay volunteer.

In Nome Noralee had a half-time job "slinging hash at the local greasy spoon," as she put it, and the money she earned at it she donated toward the purchase of office equipment for the radio station. The rest of her workday she spent doing office work and helping Father Jim wherever needed. He reported to Bishop Gleeson that Noralee was "working out fine."

In addition to Noralee, Father Jim had with him in Nome Luella Poole, his own dear mother. She had come to be with her son, but also to do the cooking.

However, he still needed someone well versed in the technical aspects of radio, some competent lay volunteer willing to dedicate two years of his life to the Nome radio apostolate. So, not long after he got his feet on the ground in Nome, he began to cast about for what he called "that key man."

Father Jim never had any intention of mastering the technical side of radio himself. He did, however, feel a need for having a broad general knowledge of this medium and for establishing contacts with various people knowledgeable in all aspects of radio. Accordingly — with Bishop Gleeson's permission — he spent the latter part of September and the first part of October traveling widely throughout the Lower 48. In New York, Minneapolis, Los Angeles, Portland, Seattle, and Anchorage he renewed old contacts, made new ones, talked radio, attended a radio seminar, searched for that key man, begged money and pledges of money, got "little collection deals going," and left behind Eskimo dolls and ivory rosaries to be raffled off to raise cash needed for his station.

A busy man when on the road? Yes! But also a busy man when at home. Hear him tell it: "Along with the radio work and planning, we also have a parish to run, a Mass each day here at the church, another each day at King Island Village, catechism, visiting the jail and the hospital regularly and being on call, keeping a swinging Teen Club from swinging too far, redecorating and remodeling the church, working on the Tourist Committee of the Chamber of Commerce, and keeping contact with Catholic students at the Vocational School."

The above quote is from the September 1966 *Nome Static*, "Transmission One," the first in the series of Father Jim's mimeographed monthly newsletters. By means of these "Transmissions" — complete with drawings of scenes out of Nome, or Arctic, or Eskimo life, and written in a direct, breezy tone of familiarity — he has over the years kept in close contact with his friends and benefactors and former volunteers. It is mainly through the *Static* that he keeps them posted on almost every aspect of his work in Nome, thanks them profusely for their support, and, unabashedly pressures them ("How about cutting some corners and giving us a hand, no matter how small!" "Can you interest someone in our project?" "We really do need your help!") to continue spurting north the money, the lifeblood, he needs to keep his radio ministry alive.

Father Jim was indeed a busy man, but also a happy, highly optimistic man during his first autumn in Nome. In that same September *Static* he expressed the confident view that a little more financial help would enable him to "put this thing over the top and on the air by '67." With the $15,000 Bishop Gleeson had obtained for him from the Society for the Propagation of the Faith, he had, by the end of 1966, the $30,000 he thought sufficient to get the station on the air.

Transmission 6

Great Expectations: 1967

Toward the end of 1967 Father Jim had radio program schedules pretty well worked out, and was scouting around for about five acres of ground on the eastern outskirts of Nome for a remote tower and transmitter site. He was also groping his way through the "mountains of paper work" involved in getting the necessary permits from the Federal Communications Commission to erect a station. But for the kind, expert help received from A.G. "Augie" Hiebert of Northern Television, Inc., Anchorage, he would have — by his own admission — gotten hopelessly lost.

"When will we be on the air? Now that is a good question!" we read in the January *Static*. We also learn from this that Noralee was now a full-time teacher at Nome's Beltz High School, and donating 100% of her paycheck toward the purchase of radio station equipment. Welcome as this financial support was, it was far from adequate for the needs of the station now on the drawing board.

"Many thanks, but please!" Beginning with the first issue of the *Static*, this two-pronged refrain has been a standard feature of virtually every transmission since. Nevertheless, in spite of its constant recurrence, it has not lost its urgent, sincere ring. Every month's donations are welcomed, in Father Jim's words, "like a monthly transfusion." And for every drop of this vital support he is genuinely grateful — and he lets his donors know it. His variations on the theme of heartfelt gratitude are almost limitless. A favorite expression of his — and a most fitting one — is *Quyaana*, the Eskimo for "thank you!"

There is irony, almost pathos, in the fact that Father Jim's begging platform should be Nome, a city founded on sands originally so rich in gold that they yielded millions, made millionaires, and led to early-day Nome's being called "the city on the golden sands, the poor man's paradise." He, however, throughout his years there, has known — financially speaking — almost nothing but hard times in paradise.

And on and on Father Jim planned and dreamed — and begged. In his March 1967 *Static* he wrote, "After eight years of planning! Yes, it has been that many years that we have been dreaming and hoping and trying to get a radio station going up in this neck of the woods. Now, this summer, we are down to the very realistic 'happening' of buying land, buying equipment, building a remote site, laying cable, remodeling an old house into a studio, and all the other tasks necessary before getting 'on the air.' So do *please* remember us at this time with your help and prayers."

Father Jim and Thunder, 1968. (Alaskan Shepherd *Collection*)

Growing — along with the radio dream — was also Father Jim's pet pooch, Thunder, a white Siberian husky, still a pup in 1967, but growing up fast. While Father Jim, his mother, and Noralee were holding down the Nome fort, Thunder was guarding it — "and looking more and more alert as he sniffed the oncoming winter." For years he was the much loved, much petted, pampered mascot of the station gang. All that was asked of him was that he wag his tail in friendly greeting whenever any of the gang came near him. For the rest, he was free to roam — at chain's length — and howl with the wolves and the blizzards. Thunder regularly received a line or two in the *Static*. His passing was solemnly mourned by the whole gang.

Father Jim's staff of volunteers also grew in 1967. John Young came in the summer to help out for a time. And in the fall Therese Burik arrived from St. Marys, where she had been a volunteer office worker, to begin a tour of generous volunteer service that was to last close to 20 years. She took over most of the office work connected with getting a station on the air and running a parish.

Therese — more commonly known as "Tweet" — was originally from Byesville, Ohio. Before coming to Alaska she was a high-positioned secretary in one of the federal offices in Washington, D.C. Her sharp business sense, along with her exceptional managerial skills, proved to be of inestimable value to Father Jim and his ministry in Nome.

Transmission 7

A Time to Build: 1968

"Our land problems up here are finally solved," wrote Father Jim — somewhat prematurely, as we shall see — in the January 1968 *Static*. That this supposed resolution of the land problem meant a great deal to him is evident from his added remark, "When we finally get on the air, I will breathe the largest sigh of relief ever let forth in

First support nurse, Betty Connors, tidying up her room, 1968. *(KNOM Collection)*

this largest state." One would think that getting a few acres of land for a tower and transmitter for an educational radio station in a state of well over half a million square miles would have been a simple matter. Not so. Before the first shovelful of dirt could be turned, mountains of paper work had to be moved.

Jesuit lay brother John Huck was on hand in the summer of 1968, and "doing a great job" remodeling the kitchen and preparing dormitory facilities for additional awaited staff. That same summer Paul Dieser — "the man with the radio brains" — too, came to Nome, to order equipment, and to set up a ham radio rig. Noralee, after serving five years as a lay volunteer, decided to continue to help Father Jim, but henceforth only on a spare-time basis.

In September Betty Connors from Boston joined the staff, and immediately began working full-time in Nome's Maynard McDougall Memorial Hospital and donating all her salary to the radio dream. Betty was the first in a long line of lay volunteer "support nurses" to work in the hospital and hand over total earnings, receiving in return only travel expenses, room and board, and a bit of pocket money. This was a new concept in lay volunteer work. Over the years nurses' salaries have supplied roughly 60% of the money needed for the day-to-day operation of the radio station.

Nurses' salaries have, unquestionably, been of the utmost importance to the station — have been nothing less than its financial backbone. At the same time the nurses themselves have profited immensely, professionally, from their work in the Nome hospital. Cases, enriching experiences they might have met up with but seldom, if ever, in large city hospitals, they have encountered early on and frequently in Nome.

Routinely nurses have played the role of flying nightingales, have made mercy flights to remote outlying villages in small bush planes to bring in sick or injured patients. As medical escorts most all have accompanied patients to the bigger hospitals in Anchorage. One delivered a baby on an emergency "Medivac" trip to Anchorage. The delivery room was an Aztec, about 10,000 feet up. "Ho-hum," wrote Father Jim, "another uneventful day." He went on to add, "Nurses often get more experience up here in a few months than they do in years elsewhere."

"This soon to be started radio station . . .," wrote Father Jim in January, when Bishop Gleeson applied for a right of way for a station transmitter site. Father Jim at the time thought the land problem solved. In March he wrote optimistically, "as we approach the goal so closely now." However, six months later he was a very frustrated man. "We are at our wits' end," he wrote, "waiting for the processing of our paper work for the radio station. But, I guess this is to be built on the foundation of patience." By this time his radio project seemed hopelessly entangled in the toils of bureaucratic red tape. In his desperation he entrusted the whole radio affair to St. Jude, patron of desperate cases.

As the year wound down, the ham radio equipment kept arriving, and many of the staff kept busy trying to earn their ham licenses.

"We are so close to the end!" On this upbeat, intriguingly ambiguous note Father Jim signed off for the year 1968.

Transmission 8

A Time to Be Patient: 1969

"One's ideas are not always blessed by all," wrote Father Jim to a priest friend in 1965. He was speaking of his radio ideas. It is not hard to detect an overtone of hurt in this laconic understatement. While he knew he had the support of Bishop Gleeson from the day he first mentioned

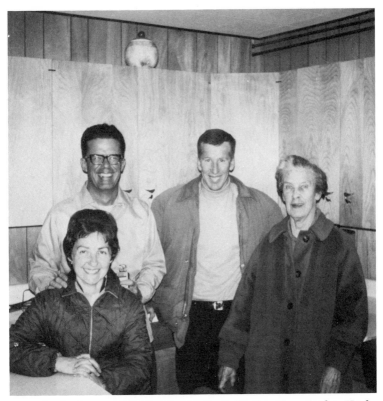

"Way back when...," 1969: Therese Burik, Father Jim, Brother Huck, Mrs. Poole. *(KNOM Collection)*

to him his plans for a radio station, he sensed a certain indifference, even opposition to it on the part of some of his fellow priests. He implied as much when on 18 February 1969 he wrote to Father Bernard F. McMeel, Superior of all the Alaska Jesuits, "If our radio station venture is to be a success, it will need the cooperation, guidance, advice, and prayers of all our padres." Some time later he wrote that it was "a real boost to the old morale to have the support and confidence of all the padres." In fairness to the "padres" he admitted that he had not always done enough to keep them informed on the progress of what he referred to as the "Alaska Radio Mission."

Father Jim spent February 1969 attending the Don Martin School of Radio in Hollywood. There he focused on announcing, newscasting, and commercial techniques. The faculty he found to be "darn nice" to him.

By March Father Jim had the capital needed to set up a radio station in the bank. The begging pitch shifted now from "to purchase" to "to run." However, much hard-to-come-by patience was still necessary as the F.C.C. first kept delaying approval of his application for the all-essential license, and then put a freeze on all applications for AM licenses.

Nevertheless, undaunted, he applied to the F.C.C. for permission to construct the new station. With his application he included a petition that the Commission waive the freeze in his case.

It is no secret that from the outset KICY felt itself threatened by the prospect of a new religious radio station in Nome, and, therefore, not surprisingly, took whatever action it could to prevent its establishment. Among other things, it filed a protest with the F.C.C., requesting that the Commission not waive the freeze in favor of the new station. KICY feared head-on competition from the rival station both in the areas of selling commercials and of "gospelizing." Its fears, while understandable, were, in reality, groundless, for the new station was to be wholly non-commercial and very limited in its religious programming. As it turned out, KICY's opposition to the petition for a waiver of the freeze brought about only a relatively short delay. A few months later the F.C.C. granted the petition. All in all, relations between the two stations have, over the years, been friendly. In times of special need they regularly come to one another's assistance.

"Man," Father Jim wrote in the July 1969 *Static*, "how long have I waited to have something on the positive side to report about my first love, radio! We just received a 'memorandum, opinion, and order' from the F.C.C. granting our petition for a waiver of the freeze. Our application for an AM license has now been accepted for filing. The largest of all the hurdles is behind us...We are getting down to 'show and tell' in the very near future." On 15 September the Commission informed him that it was processing his application with a view to granting a construction permit.

With radio his first love, and the Nome parish his primary responsibility, Father Jim — ever a conscientious pastor — was, understandably, torn between the two. In addition to Nome, he had charge also of Teller and Little Diomede Island when these were without an assigned priest. However, singularly blessed with competent volunteer help, he was able to carry out his twofold mission without serious hurt to either. The year 1969 brought with it significant change in regard to volunteer personnel.

Betty Connors — "a little Irish gal with a mile of smile and a heart big as Boston harbor" — returned to Boston in June. Bunny Philibert worked successfully in the parish throughout the summer. The kids loved her. After six years of most competent, unstinting volunteer work, Tweet Burik went south for a break. However, in mid-August nurses Jeannie Stoklosa and Ann Legan came north from Boston to work in the Nome hospital and donate their entire salaries to the radio venture. And in September the 69-year-old and much loved Father Harold J. Greif, S.J., arrived to begin what was to be over a decade of priestly service in Nome and outlying stations. Providence Sister Paula Cosko came from Seattle to take charge of the catechetical program, and Kathy Prueher came from Eureka, California, to take over as secretary.

In the November *Static* we read, "The big question: When do we get the green light to go ahead on the station? We are awaiting word from the Federal Communications Commission and also from the Bureau of Land Management. It seems we have been waiting about ten years, but actually only five." As the year 1969 ended, Father Jim was still waiting for "that big final word."

Sister Paula Cosko, S.P., with some of her little charges, 1971. *(Photo by Tom Busch)*

Transmission 9

Washington Says "Go!": 1970

With the dawning of the new year 1970, Brother Huck, accompanied by Leigh Birkeland from Minnesota, returned to Nome to do carpentry work on the rectory and to install a new, much needed heating system. Brother Huck left in February, but soon thereafter Tom Karlin came from Kansas to help carry on the work of maintenance and remodeling. Tom's carpentry and cabinetwork have been praised as being of the very finest workmanship.

The tide of high hopes surged again early in the year. "Letters coming in," wrote Father Jim in the February *Static*, "from U.S. Senator Ted Stevens and Secretary of the Interior Walter Hickel, and others. All seem very, very

The KNOM studio, April 1970, about two weeks into construction. *(Photo by Tom Busch)*

encouraging about the prospects of our very soon getting that construction permit for the station and finally getting the show on the road."

At this point, enter "that key man!" From Station WLDB in Atlantic City, New Jersey, in February, with his first class radio license still fresh, came, to serve as chief engineer for the design and construction of the station, Boston College graduate Thomas Anthony Busch. After Father Jim, Tom is the one man to whom the station owes more than to any other. He would dispute that, however. Augie Hiebert, Tom maintains, "is probably the person most responsible for the radio station project reaching fruition."

"The green light signal to go ahead," Father Jim wrote in April, "is very close now, and we are getting excited." The radio project was still being held up because permits for station construction and right of way for the tower and transmitter building were not yet in hand. Only Washington could grant the required permits and right of way. Senator Stevens in Washington was doing all he could to get the light on green. "So things are looking up," Father Jim wrote in May, "and who knows but before the next letter comes your way, we may have the 'go!' signal — after all these months and years of waiting!"

To join Busch, Birkeland, and Karlin, Brother Huck returned in June, bringing with him Brother Marion Melius, S.J., and lay volunteer John Schuessler. This skilled, in-house construction crew made rapid progress on the remodeling of the building that was to house the planned station and part of the staff — the old James Walsh home, a two-story structure near St. Joseph's Church. Before long, the downstairs of this building was transformed into a very adequate studio suite (designed by Tom Busch), the upstairs into a men's dorm.

By this time volunteer nurse Carol Cockrill from Peoria, Illinois, too, was part of "the gang."

With "WASHINGTON SAYS 'GO!'!!!!!" Father Jim banner headlined the July 1970 *Static*. "The happiest greetings in the world!" After so much waiting and frustration on his part, his exuberance is surely understandable. He and his radio family were at dinner, when Bishop Robert L. Whelan, S.J. — Father Jim's former high school teacher and now Bishop Gleeson's successor — telephoned him the long-awaited news that the F.C.C. in Washington had granted the construction permit.

This construction permit was just that; it was not a radio license. It merely granted permission to go ahead and build the station, equip it, put up a tower and get ready to broadcast. This done, there were to follow several months

Brother John Huck, S.J., and Tom Karlin watch the yearly Nome River Raft Race, 1968. *(KNOM Collection)*

to test transmissions. If, and when, these checked out to the satisfaction of the F.C.C., the license to go on the air with regular broadcasting would be granted.

The day after the good news was received, long lists of equipment orders — orders that had been lying in readiness for months — went into the mail. Before the day was over, orders totaling almost $60,000 had been placed. As was to be expected, actual costs far exceeded earlier estimates. "Big dent in our bank account," summarized Father Jim. It was a dent, however, that caused little pain.

Buildings were being remodeled and upgraded, and equipment was on order, but more manpower was still needed. A nationwide search for four men with "high ideals and a desire to help others, good radio personality with announcing experience, willing to work as a volunteer without pay" was intensified.

In August — accompanied both by sad farewells from the radio crew and high praise from the hospital administra-

Father Jim posing in 1970 with King Island Eskimo girl, Marilyn Koezuna, later a KNOM announcer, and a King Island Eskimo boy. *(Photo by Tom Busch)*

tion, doctors, and grateful patients — nurses Jeannie Stoklosa and Ann Legan departed for Boston. (A bit of KNOM in-house trivia that will interest volunteers of the 70s: It was Ann who named the "Hosey Chart," use of which continued for at least a decade. Father Jim developed that wall chart to keep track of how often individuals washed dishes. It was his attempt to equalize the burden of that chore. Ann named it "Hosey Chart" after the word "hosey," which she claimed was Bridgewater, Mass., slang for "dibs" or "claim.") Soon thereafter, however, Ida Schilter from Eatonville, Washington, arrived to help carry on with the nursing and supporting. About this time, too, Jack Carr came from Salt Lake City to serve as general maintenance man at the Nome parish and radio station. Jack is fondly remembered for doing "a great job at repairing much with not much." He was soon followed by Jesuit lay brother Randy McIlvain, mechanic and jack of many trades, and volunteer Terry McMahon.

Powder monkey Sam Tucker packing a charge of dynamite into the permafrost to enlarge the pier hole for the main tower's SW guy wire. *(Photo by Tom Busch)*

**Utility Tower Company crew members erecting the 236-foot KNOM tower,
28 October 1970.** *(Photo by Tom Busch)*

The construction permit from the F.C.C. was dated 29 June, but it was not until 9 September that the Bureau of Land Management gave authorized issuance of the right of way at the transmitter site — seemingly. As it turned out, it was not until 5 October that it actually gave the go ahead, and then only tentatively. Nevertheless, the race against winter was on, and on 11 September Busch and recent addition to the Nome radio team, six-foot-five radio announcer and engineer John Pfeifer from Wichita, Kansas, "tore right into digging a tower foundation." This was easier said than done.

For the main tower foundation a hole seven feet square and fifteen feet deep had to be dug in ground permanently frozen. Three holes for guy wires were also needed. After the insulating mat of tundra vegetation had been removed, the ground — a mixture of frozen silt and muck — looked, according to Busch, "like a chocolate skating rink." This permanently frozen subsoil, technically known as "permafrost," was so resilient that half the time the vigorously swung pick simply bounced right back to its swinger.

After five days of chipping away with little progress to show, and time running out, the digging duo called for help. Powder monkey Sam Tucker answered the call. He gave them 3-foot long chisels, which they heated to red hot in driftwood fires and then pounded into the permafrost to melt out a hole big enough for a charge of dynamite. Sam then packed the hole with sticks of dynamite, lit the fuse, mumbled the customary "Fire in the hole!" and casually walked away. "Sssssszzzzzzzzup!" — and chunks of frozen terra firma thudded down.

"John and I," wrote Tom, "would work in different holes, either sledge hammering or bucketing out the rubble. After we got the main hole eight feet down, it took two of us to clear out the junk, one shoveling into a bucket, the other hauling it up.

"We went at a relentless pace. Up at 7, out to work, a quick sandwich for lunch, back home at 6 — and often back to the site after dinner for a couple extra hours. The weather went from mild to nippy, and the tundra started getting crunchy with frost."

When the main hole was thought finished, it was measured and found to be almost a foot short both in width and depth. To widen and deepen it, picking was tried. This did not work. An old-timers' trick was suggested: fill the hole with driftwood, pour in a couple gallons of gasoline, step back, toss in a lighted torch.

"Woof!" continues Tom's account. "Our hole burned all day and all night, and the permafrost sides did slough off. But to our horror, we were left with a 6-foot deep hole, filled below that level with wet mud and half-burned timbers."

The entire radio crew came out and helped, one after another, all one Sunday, from dawn to well after sunset, bucketing out the muck. By the end of the day the hole was ready. On Monday Karlin put in the concrete forms; on Tuesday concrete was poured and left to cure for a week. Frost was predicted. Out of old doors, scrap lumber, tin and plastic sheeting canopies were built to cover the four piers. Kerosene smudge pots were placed under the canopies to keep the temperature above freezing.

It snowed a few inches, and there was great concern that winter weather would soon put an end to outdoor operations. It was by now mid-October.

The previous August the question was raised as to whether or not local people should be given the job of erecting the transmitter tower. This would have meant a saving of five thousand hard-begged dollars. However, the radio experts consulted by Father Jim about the matter all warned him against "a homemade operation," and urged him to get professionals to do the job. Accordingly, the Utility Tower Company was hired to come to Nome and put up the tower. By the end of December the 236-foot tower was up, and everything at the site was ready to go.

In late October, Tweet — armed now with a third class

radio license, so that she could be "the weather girl" — returned to take up her old position, that of Business Manager of the station.

Of Tweet, Tom Busch wrote, "To those of us who didn't know her, Tweet was a legend. She soon became a dear friend. It's a burdensome label to be called indispensable to KNOM, but Tweet deserves the phrase as much as anyone." No one acquainted with her contribution to the station over the years will dispute that.

KNOM — there we finally have it! "K" as in "Kay," "NOM" as in "NOMe." That gives us both K-N-O-M and "Kay-Nome." Turn your dial to 780 kilohertz on your AM receiver and hear, "This is KayNome, Alaska!" or "This is K-N-O-M, Nome, Alaska!" Credit Tom Busch and serendipity for this felicitous choice of call letters!

The call letters had to start with "K" and consist of four letters. K-R-S-T, "Christ," and K-O-R-R, "Heart Radio," in honor of the Sacred Heart, had been proposed. But, being a natural, KNOM won out — but not all that easily. Father Jim accepted it only with a certain reluctance. He had reservations about the station's being so strongly associated with Nome, rather than with the villages. It is interesting to note that, when he applied for the call letters KNOM, he learned, at first, that they were not available, having been assigned, as they were, to the Coast Guard cutter *Chiquimula*. However, as the vessel had been abandoned some time before, the Coast Guard relinquished the use of "KNOM" to the station.

Bad health forced Leigh Birkeland to leave for his home in Minnesota at the end of October. The following month Carol Cockrill — after doing "a really great job" — finished her time of volunteer work and took her leave. To replace her RN Kitty Orris came from McKeesport, Pennsylvania. And on 30 November Alex Hills arrived from Sparta, New Jersey, to serve as an engineer and radio announcer. Alex came with a newly grown beard, a pair of skis, a degree in Electrical Engineering, and a Master of Science degree.

To do volunteer work in Nome, he passed up an opportunity to build power transmission lines in South America.

"We have 92 educational spots to produce," wrote Father Jim in the December 1970 *Static*, "before we are on the air SOME TIME IN JANUARY!" And on that highly optimistic note he ended the year.

Transmission 10

Glitches and Headaches: 1971a

On New Year's Eve some of the volunteers rang the big bell in the church steeple loud and long to welcome in what was to be a watershed year in the lives of Father Jim and his crew, the year 1971. Spirits ran high. The KNOMers had just celebrated "a fantastic Christmas" — live tree and all.

It has all along, even during hard times, been a set policy with Father Jim that all feasts, holidays, birthdays, special occasions — whether sacred or secular — be joyous, family celebrations for the KNOM gang. The great Church feasts are always celebrated with especially well prepared liturgies, followed by festive meals, generally cooked by Tweet.

Christmases in particular have been the highlight events of every year. The big day is anticipated and prepared for throughout the preceding four weeks not only in the liturgies of Advent, but also by means of KNOM's own special Kris Kringle custom.

Right after Thanksgiving each member of the staff picks a name out of a box, and all during Advent gives little presents to, prepares little surprises for, the person whose name he or she drew. On Christmas day — following the sumptuous Tweet-cooked dinner — the Christmas tree ceremony takes place. At this everyone receives — among other gifts — a regular present from his or her Kris Kringle, whose identity is now revealed. "It's a really fun experience," according to Father Jim, "a lot of laughs and a fine welder of community spirit. It's hard to imagine a warmer spirit of loving and giving than in this community."

In the January 1971 *Static* we read, "Well, when do

we go on the air?" In answer to the question — coming at him from all sides — Father Jim wrote, "The closest we can say is that by the time you get the next *Nome Static* we will be on the air! It looks very much like the first week in February right now."

By early February the whole studio complex was finished, and Brother Huck and John Schuessler were on their way to St. Marys to work there. Terry McMahon, who helped with the building of the station, also left at this time. Shortly after their departures, nurse Sally Duggan from Queens, New York, arrived. She was soon followed by radio announcer Leo Kehs from Bethlehem, Pennsylvania, and newsman Harry Gallagher from Bala Cynwyd, Pennsylvania.

By late February Father Jim could still write only, "I would love to say we are on the air." But — more delays, more waiting, more drain on the personal patience bank continued to be the order of the day. Two pieces of equipment having to do with metering were still not on hand. The agony of waiting was only intensified by the premature letters of greetings and congratulations that had already started to come from various prominent dignitaries. "Remember way back," a frustrated Father Jim asked rhetorically, "when there was such a thing as patience?"

However, sometime in March KNOM was actually "on the air" — kind of. The station was test broadcasting daily for 30 minutes, and getting favorable signal reports from the target area. At St. Marys especially, KNOM received great attention. People were excited in a personal sense for Father Jim, and they would run from house to house to see if their friends had heard KNOM broadcasting.

The first song ever played over KNOM — played solely for testing purposes — was a repeating, continuous loop cartridge of Susan Raye's "L.A. International Airport." Two other testing songs played into the ground on continuous loop cartridges were "If You Could Read My Mind," by Gordon Lightfoot, and "Snowbird," by Anne Murray. (This

KNOM Staff 1971. (Left to Right), First Row: Fr. Jim Poole, S.J., Manager; Tom Busch, Engineer; John Pfeifer, Announcer; Jack Carr, Maintenance; Harry Gallagher, Newsman; Second Row: Leo Kehs, Announcer; Kathy Prueher, Secretary; Mrs. Poole, Cook and "Mother"; Alex Hills, Announcer; Therese "Tweet" Burik, Business Manager; Third Row: Kitty Orris, R.N., Support Nurse; Sally Duggan, R.N., Support Nurse; Fr. Harold Greif, S.J., Associate Pastor; Sister Paula Cosko, S.P., Parish Religious Instructor; Ida Schilter, R.N., Support Nurse. One more nurse, Helen Osdieck; a radio man, Don Pike; an Assistant Cook, Lucy Schilter; and Secretary, Carol Razewski, are expected soon. (Photo by George Sabo)

latter was a special favorite of Mrs. Poole's.) Response from the field to the testing was encouraging, but some letter writers — not recognizing the testing for what it was — wondered whether the station couldn't possibly, please, change records a little more often.

The radio station was, Father Jim admitted, "this very favorite project of ours." Still, it would be quite false to conclude that it was his sole, all-consuming concern. He was all the while also the pastor of the Nome parish, with all that that entails. At the same time he was a member of the Nome Chamber of Commerce, of the Alaska Christian Conference, of the Rotarians, and head of the Housing Board. He worked with the Boy Scouts, the King Teens, the Sub-Teens, the Receiving Home, the Alcoholism Center, the Community Center. He served on the Nome Arts Council, and on the Alaska State Council on the Arts — for a time as vice-chairman of this latter. Later he became very active in the Marriage Encounter movement. "Just a few things to take up the extra slack in time," he wrote.

When asked the simple question whether Father Jim neglected his parish responsibilities because of his seeming preoccupation with radio, one of his parishioners came to his defense, rather aggressively — as if he had been maliciously, falsely charged with neglect. She insisted that she knew of no complaints against him on this account, that, on the contrary, he was always a very devoted pastor.

It was by working overtime, in overdrive, and by firing up his support cast with his own infectious enthusiasm that he was able to keep going and accomplish so much. In many respects the parish actually profited from its radio connection. Routinely members of the radio corps help out with the music and singing in the church, with the teaching of Christian Doctrine, with youth work, with cleaning and maintenance — and, in a general way, simply by being active, involved members of the parish community.

"You know," Father Jim began the April *Static*, "I'm getting rather ashamed to write another newsletter and still not be on the air. When we actually get on the air, I do believe the shock will be too much for me."

In May "all sorts of glitches and headaches" still plagued the station. Understandably, Father Jim found this "most discouraging. There just isn't any patience left anymore." Throughout the waiting ordeal he was sustained in very large measure by the unabated dedication of his volunteer staff. "No matter how discouraging things get," he wrote, "they stay right in there, working with all they have."

That same May, Father Jim, S.J., became also Father Jim, D.J. — when he took and passed his radio exam and received his shiny new third class radiotelephone license.

Kathy Prueher, after putting in two years as a competent, devoted secretary, left in June for her home in California. She missed the big day, that so long awaited sign-on day, by just one month.

Transmission 11

Sign-On: 1971b

In spite of the various technical problems that kept cropping up in the spring of 1971, Father Jim felt that an official sign-on day should be set and announced. Some of his staff had reservations about this being done. He insisted, and Wednesday, 14 July 1971, was selected as KNOM's first broadcast day.

A week or so before the first broadcast, all the equipment was "purring and ready to go," according to Tom Busch. However, the designated announcers — not having been on the air for a year or more — were a little nervous

Bishop Robert Whelan pushes the button to start KNOM's inaugural program, 14 July 1971. Father Jim and volunteers look on. (*Photo by George Sabo*)

and rusty. To ease nerves and to take the rust off, Tom strung a public address wire from the studio to the rectory, and for a solid week they pretended they were actually on the air as they programmed sixteen hours a day into the rectory speaker. The dry run had its desired effects.

With everyone and everything finally set to "hit the air-ways," the crew did a last-day test of the transmitter on the 13th, just as it had done for months. Panic! "Before any of us realized it," recalled Busch, "the beast burned through a copper strap in the tuning box, and remained transmitting without an antenna. The transmitter was damaged. Six tiny resistors were destroyed. No one in Nome had anything close to replacements, and the transmitter wouldn't work without 'em. We were due to sign on in 24 hours."

Fortunately, Kitty Orris, who had just flown to Anchorage on a medical mission, was able to pick up the dollar's worth of parts and hand carry them to Nome the afternoon of sign-on day. Less than three hours before "the big moment," all systems were again go.

A week before sign-on, the question arose: How to let people know the station was about to go on the air, so that they would not miss the grand opening? John Pfeifer had the answer and he knew how to lend drama to the historic moment. He rushed into the production studio, plopped a Baby Ben alarm clock into the wastebasket with a microphone, and recorded a half-hour countdown, with the sound of the ticking between time announcements.

Before the countdown began, the male crew got all dressed up in coats and ties, the women in party dresses. The whole staff then gathered in the studio to watch as Bishop Whelan — legal owner of the station — blessed the station and asked God's blessings on all the generous people who helped make it possible.

At 4:29 P.M. all held their breath as Father Jim pushed the ON/RAISE button. At 4:30, Pfeifer's tape went on the air with "This is KNOM, Nome, Alaska, operating under

The KNOM crew pose in Studio A on the first day, 14 July 1971. (Left to Right) Bishop Robert Whelan, S.J., Fr. Jim Poole, S.J., Leo Kehs (Evening Announcer), Therese "Tweet" Burik (Business Manager), Tom Busch (Chief Engineer/Announcer), Luella Poole (Fr. Jim's mother), Harry Gallagher (News Director), Fr. Harold Greif, S.J., Ida Schilter (Support Nurse), Mark Joshu (a volunteer visiting from Bethel), Tom Karlin (Supervisor of Building Construction), Alex Hills (Engineer/Announcer), John Pfeifer (Engineer/Announcer), Bro. John Huck, S.J., (Construction), Dennis Pikonganna (a King Islander who helped with construction), and John Schuessler (who painted and carpeted the studio). *(Photo by George Sabo)*

program test authority of the Federal Communications Commission. KNOM will sign on the air in 30 minutes." Then, as each minute ticked by, his voice was heard over the still air: "29...28...27..." At the next 10-minute interval, "twenty minutes before KNOM goes on the air." Finally, he was down to the last minute. And exactly at 5:00, Bishop Whelan pushed the tape recorder START button that began the inaugural program with the voice of Leo Kehs: "Announcing the world's newest radio station! This is KNOM, Nome, Alaska!" With these brief sign-on words the station declared its birth.

After the fanfare, what next? was the question facing Tom Busch shortly before sign-on day. By drawing the short straw, Tom got stuck with producing KNOM's hour-long opening program. John Pfeifer suggested the station go right into its theme song, "We've Only Just Begun," by the Carpenters. (It was his idea that this song be KNOM's theme song.) After the music, John reasoned, the pressure would be less, and messages of congratulations could then be played in whatever order was thought suitable. The suggestion was a good one, and Tom chose to act on it. However, the theme song agreed on was on none of the records in the station's still severely limited record library. After much casting about, a record with the song was finally located. It was owned by first grade teacher Merriel Balazy, who graciously loaned it to the station for the day. The song had its nerve-quieting effect. (Incidentally, it continued to be, and still is, KNOM's theme song, and Father Jim's in particular.)

"Needless to say," wrote Father Jim, "the first few minutes were nervous ones; but, as the show progressed, everyone relaxed, and soon the mood was about at cloud nine."

There was then a quick adjournment to the upstairs office for a champagne celebration, followed by sittings for official staff photos by George Sabo.

For some months now messages had been coming into the station from around the world, and for the remainder of that memorable sign-on day these were read out over the 780 kilocycle AM station. A taped message from Pope Paul VI read: "On this occasion we are happy to send our greetings to our dear sons and daughters in Alaska. Grace and peace from God our Father and from the Lord Jesus Christ. You are in our thoughts and prayers, and we assure you all of our deep affection. By means of the radio we are happy to have the opportunity to send our special blessing into your homes. It goes to the young, to the old, to orphans, to the children, to the sick, to all those who love us in faith. May almighty God bless..."

From the White House President Richard M. Nixon sent greetings and congratulations, and informed Father Jim that he was "particularly pleased to learn about Alaska's new educational oriented radio station."

Congratulatory messages and best wishes had been received also from such notables as U.S. Senators from Alaska Mike Gravel and Ted Stevens, Congressman Nick Begich, Alaska Governor William Egan, Bing Crosby, and Bob Hope. These, too, were heard throughout western Alaska over KNOM on 14 July 1971.

Don Pike the week after "sign-on." *(Photo by George Sabo)*

From the outset KNOM's signal was heard loud and clear, far and wide, by the very people — approximately 30,000 — Father Jim had hoped most to reach: the Eskimos and Indians living in 90-some isolated villages, fish camps, and trapping camps scattered across the tundra, along the Bering Sea coast, and along the rivers and sloughs of western Alaska. Situated, as it is, on the coast of the Bering Sea, Nome commands the air waves not only to the offshore islands and to the vast deltas of the Yukon and Kuskokwim Rivers, but also to the interior regions of western Alaska. Nome is noted for having a very good sounding board for signals, for its excellent "on water transmissions."

Contributing also to KNOM's strong, crisp clear-channel signal is the quality of its equipment. While KNOM was still nothing more than an airy dream, Father Jim was already convinced that only the best radio equipment available would be good enough for the station. Given the high freight rates — owing to the station's remoteness — and the prohibitive costs of flying in emergency maintenance experts, it would be folly, he reasoned, to assemble any but the best, the most reliable equipment money could buy. He felt, too, that the poor of western Alaska deserved the best that daring and dedication could bring them.

KNOM went on the air with all new equipment, manufactured — with few exceptions — by Collins Radio and Moseley Associates. Its 10,000-watt Collins 820F-1 transmitter is located on the tundra about three miles east of Nome. Next to it stands the 236-foot antenna tower with a folded unipole configuration that makes the tower, in effect, as good as one over 300 feet. Over this the KNOM high-fidelity signal goes out to cover a listening area of 146,000 square miles. Under rare, exceptionally favorable conditions the station can be received in places as far away as New Zealand.

Despite the quality of the equipment used, and despite all the care the KNOM crew had put into constructing the station, only five days after signing on, the station

Harry Gallagher, KNOM's first news director. *(Photo by George Sabo)*

suffered a major setback, had to go off the air. On Monday, 19 July, RCA Alascom complained that nondirectional KNOM was transmitting a spurious signal on 500 khz, the international distress frequency. Almost immediately, voluntarily the station signed off. Things were, understandably, "a little gloomy around the station." However, without delay, consulting engineer John Mullaney was flown in from Washington, D.C., and under his guidance the crew installed special filters, and within seven days had KNOM back on the air again. John was so won over to the whole radio mission cause that he waived the originally agreed upon $250 per day consultant's fee and became a regular donor to KNOM ever after.

Here should be mentioned also Joe Hennessey, Esq., the Washington, D.C., communications attorney who has contributed his services to KNOM at no charge from the very beginning. Joe helped right from the time of the original application, through every license renewal, and with many problems in between. Like consulting engineer John Mullaney, rather than charge for his services, Joe is a faithful benefactor.

"Finally, we're on the air, in business, settled down to the job we have been planning for nine years!" wrote Father Jim in late July. He had never doubted — though at times his patience was severely tried — that one day his dream would be realized.

Again, what manner of man is Father Jim that he can conceive, undertake, and bring to fruition a project of the magnitude and complexity of the whole KNOM operation? For all his dreaming, he is an eminently practical man, a man with real charisma when it comes to marshaling resources, igniting people with his own upbeat enthusiasm for a cause. Archbishop Francis T. Hurley of Anchorage described him as "a dynamic priest, a man of personal discipline despite his relaxed, almost casual manner."

Transmission 12
Programming for Western Alaska: 1971c

The day KNOM began broadcasting, Father Jim stated the main, threefold purpose of the station as: "(1) to help in any way we can the people of western Alaska to bridge the gap between the old ways and the new; (2) to help especially the young people today in building a character that is strong enough to face up to all of the problems they meet in their lives; (3) plain old enjoyment, to bring a little bit of sunshine and happiness into many homes."

By August Father Jim and his versatile staff found that KNOM — "Yours for western Alaska!" — had enjoyment and happiness to offer not only for its listening audience, but for its staff as well, that running a radio station could actually be "a lot of fun." He himself had four sessions a day of religious programming, and a 5-hour Saturday Afternoon Show. Alex Hills, Tom Busch, John Pfeifer, and Leo Kehs each had his own daily 4-hour disk-jockey style show.

Money may be the lifeblood of a radio station, but the ultimate success of a station is its ability to win and hold a listening audience. Father Jim knew this as well as anyone. And from the very outset he saw, too, that his proposed station, being essentially an educational station, would be faced with a formidable challenge in this regard. The big question: How to get listeners and keep them listening?

From the day he first began planning the station, he was firmly persuaded that to attract and hold listeners — and at the same time to "inspire" and "educate" them — he would have to mix the useful with the pleasant. His stated hope was "to get across all of the ideas with as little pain as possible." To do this he came up with a rather novel programming concept, a "soft-sell approach," as he termed it. He would use what in radio parlance are called "spots."

These spots are short and to the point, less than a minute long, never preachy, nondenominational messages of inspiration, of information. Many are styled in an easy-to-take dramatic form. Sometimes the voices used in making them are those of local Eskimos. KNOM spots fall into various categories: spiritual priorities, economy, value of prayer, sanitation, Christ's law of love, health, child care, youth, social problems, character formation, general education. There are spots dealing with antifreeze, with staying in school, with selfishness. One tells how an oyster turns an irritating grain of sand into a precious pearl.

Here are two examples:

Inspirational
Please be careful how you throw your words around. There are many hearts so easily broken. And of all fragile things, the human heart is the hardest to repair.

Educational
Hi, I'm down here in this galvanized metal container to remind you that one of the commonest causes of sickness in Alaska is drinking dirty water. Lots of times people keep water inside of dirty containers, with no lids. It's best to keep drinking water clean, and in barrels like the one I'm standing in.

As a general rule a spot is played every two records. At any given time 64 different spots are alternating on the air. One fourth are changed every week. As many as 200 spots may be aired on a given day. This means spot production is a major staff concern.

Many of the spots produced by Father Jim have been used by other stations all over the U.S. and by Armed Forces Radio overseas. For its inspirational spots KNOM won a Gabriel Certificate of Merit in 1981, as well as the Alaska Press Club's highest honor, the Public Service Award for 1984.

Are the spots effective? "When a youngster asks when I'm going to change one of the spots because it is so old and he rattles it off almost verbatim," says Father Jim with a gleam in his eyes, "I know he got the message."

To make the spots palatable, to immunize against the "turn-off syndrome," they are mixed in with attractive programming consisting mainly of newscasts, regular features, public service segments, ad hoc interviews, and recorded music.

The music, the mainstay of KNOM's programming, has always been mostly half easy-listening — contemporary and "oldies" — and half country-western. Until the late 1970s KNOM played rock music from 3:00 to 5:00 P.M. The program was moved to 7:00 to 9:00 P.M. when a survey conducted by Steve Havilland indicated that that would be a more appropriate time. In large part it has been the music that has kept KNOM's audience tuned in.

News, too, has all along been an attractive part of KNOM's daily programming, and one or two staff members devote full time to news gathering and editing. News is broadcast on the hour, with several 15-minute summaries daily. Emphasis is on local and regional news. This is gathered by telephone and in the field by the news staff. An Associated Press wire has kept the station in touch with happenings around the world. Over the years KNOM has also at various times been an affiliate of two national radio networks.

Concerning KNOM's sources of news, other than local, Tom Busch summarized in December 1984:

"Full-time network service was not available in Nome before the use of satellites.

"KNOM joined stations in Anchorage and Fairbanks in bringing up four Mutual Network newscasts a day, starting in late 1974. In December 1975 we got Mutual full-time. We would have preferred the fledgling A.P. Radio, but the service was not available in Alaska.

"Mutual never fit KNOM's news philosophy. KNOM is issue-oriented, and sensitive. Though we do fully report disaster, assault, murder, fire and flood, we do it with sensitivity. Mutual, on the other hand, leans to the sensational.

"Moreover, Mutual had a minute of commercial time inside its 5-minute hourly newscast, reducing the hourly news to four minutes, and requiring us to overlay with a public service announcement. In the late 70s, they added a second commercial minute toward the end of their 'cast, returning for a short 'kicker' story, forcing us to dump out after only 2½ minutes of news. We didn't like it, but we were stuck with it.

"Mutual was about to go off the Alascom satellite in December 1981, and it turned out that the Associated Press Radio Network was available at a price we could afford. We began A.P. in late December. The honeymoon with A.P. Radio still isn't over.

"KNOM has had more than its share of network signal outages, as the A.P. signal takes a path so circuitous that the hourly time tone, travelling at the speed of light, takes fully two-thirds of a second to reach us!

"A.P. Radio is uplinked from Virginia to Westar IV, downlinked in Los Angeles, microwaved to San Francisco, cabled to Point Reyes, uplinked to Satcom V, downlinked to Talkeetna, microwaved to Anchorage and back, re-uplinked to Satcom V, and, finally, downlinked at the Alascom earth station in Nome."

KNOM is for many listeners the primary source of information. This puts a heavy responsibility on the station. Therefore, according to Father Jim, "Accuracy, quantity, quality — to inform, educate, and inspire: this is the cornerstone of KNOM's news department." While the station does report "the ugly," it will not sensationalize it. KNOM News takes pride in accenting the pleasant. "It is the good side of each individual, indeed of society," he wrote, "which needs to be noted." Over the years the news staff has worked up ten pages of news guidelines, detailing the KNOM news philosophy.

Long before KNOM was a viable reality, Father Jim saw Church-related radio as essentially an apostolic enterprise, a microphone ministry. From the day the station went on the air, some religious broadcasting has always been among its regular features. Daily, after sign-on, the station raises its voice in morning prayer. The voice is that of Father Jim, a rich, mellow reassuring baritone voice. In the course of the day there are several inspirational talks, short helpful homilies. Every Sunday the 10-o'clock Mass goes out over the air.

Regular features include also various readings. Whole books have been serialized and read over the air, books like Poldine Carlo's *Nulato: An Indian Life on the Yukon;* William A. Oquilluk's *People of Kauwerak;* and Louis L. Renner's *Pioneer Missionary to the Bering Strait Eskimos: Bellarmine Lafortune, S.J.*

Catholic radio station KNOM in Nome brings Sunday Mass, daily morning and evening prayer, news, entertainment, weather reports, inspirational, educational and spiritual messages to listeners throughout western Alaska. *(KNOM Collection)*

"Joe's Stomach," from *Reader's Digest*, has been read. On the Children's Story Hour, Eskimo and Indian kiddies have heard about "Goldilocks and the Three Nanooks." (*Nanook* is the Eskimo for a polar bear.) Featured, too, has been "Anthropology with Dr. William J. Loyens, S.J., Professor of Anthropology at the University of Alaska." Readings and lectures are chosen with a view to helping Native people adapt to modern society while at the same time maintain their traditional Native cultures, take pride in them and in themselves.

Other regular features include also such general interest shorts as "NASA Space Notes" and "Sixty Seconds of Science." Brother Normand Berger's spots, "Native Heritage," exploring Native history and lifestyle and how traditional values apply in modern times — his "Alaska Science Forum," and his "Northwest Community College Word of the Day" — a set of 366 spots in the three main Eskimo languages spoken within KNOM's listening area have all been awarded a Distinguished Journalism Citation by the Scripps-Howard Foundation. In presenting the award, Foundation president Matt Meyer commended the station for "meritorious efforts in dealing with the assimilation of Alaskan Natives into American life." The Foundation has also honored "KNOM Encyclopedia," a series of 800 one-minute treatments of a variety of subjects, produced by Tom Busch.

KNOM has distinguished itself also by the public service that it has rendered. As soon as it went on the air, it offered daily a "hotline" program. Within a short time the station was receiving so many messages that a second daily hotline program had to be added. The program — a kind of bulletin board of the air — enables people to communicate in matters urgent and non-urgent. At times the programs carry messages highly personal, or uniquely Alaskan: "David, I will marry you May 1. Signed Mary." or, "Tell Bobby I miss him, and he should study hard." or, "I will be coming by plane tomorrow; please meet me at the field with my plane fare."

In the interest of public service KNOM News has carried — from gavel to gavel — legislative meetings, city council and school board meetings, and the like. The station regularly broadcasts job openings. KNOM's community involvement is such that it even announces the menus for the schools in the villages. It invites doctors, dentists, fish and game personnel, Native health aides, village corporation representatives and many others to share skills and interests with the KNOM radio audience.

No one will ever know whether or not KNOM has actually saved lives. It may well have — with its daily weather, marine, tide, ice advisories and updates. In an area known for its unpredictable weather patterns, its violent winds and waves, these frequent advisories and updates are very much appreciated, especially by the bush pilot flying along the coast or through the Seward Peninsula mountains, as well as by the walrus hunter or the salmon fisherman out on the Bering Sea in his open boat.

Also very much appreciated — both by the flying public and the bush airlines — are KNOM's daily public service flight information broadcasts. These keep people in the outlying villages posted on the comings and goings of the bush planes. Where weather is uncertain, flights likewise are uncertain; and this can cause great inconvenience both to pilots and to waiting, would-be passengers.

To show their gratitude to the station — especially to the "morning people" on the air — for getting out flight information, area airlines (Alaska Airlines, Bering Air, Cape Smythe Air, Foster Aviation, Harold's Air Service, Hermans Air, Munz Northern Airlines, Ryan Air, Seward Peninsula Flying Service, and Wien Airlines) have frequently offered KNOM staffers free, "courtesy," rides to the widely-scattered villages. Equipped with recorders and lots of cassettes, they enthusiastically take off to get acquainted with the villages and villagers they serve on the air, to get news stories and conduct interviews, to see bush Alaska.

In 1968, while talking with radio people in Anchorage,

Father Jim was told that after one year on the air his program format would change beyond recognition. This he believed at the time. However, while KNOM has grown with the times, its basic program format and programming philosophy have remained remarkably constant over the years. This prolonged relative sameness must be attributed to Father Jim's sound, clear, initial vision as to what KNOM was to be all about. Through the years his mind has remained open on the subject of programming, but he has seen no reason for significant change in this matter, being convinced, as he has been, that he has had KNOM on the right wavelength from the outset.

With KNOM on the air, and routine rather than crisis being the order of the day, Father Jim's chief concern was now money and staff to keep the whole operation going.

KNOM is wholly non-commercial, and never asks for money on the air. The real begging is done in virtually every "Transmission" of the *Nome Static*. In the *Static*, too, Father Jim puts out feelers for staff; but it is mainly through ads in professional journals that he recruits the help needed for his radio mission.

Nurses were first recruited through the *American Journal of Nursing*. They are now recruited through the Jesuit Volunteer Corps headquartered in Portland, Oregon. Secretarial and kitchen help also is recruited and screened mostly through the J.V.C. The same holds true now also for radio personnel. Earlier ads were placed in *Broadcasting* magazine. "Wanted," read one ad, "young men with ideals, who will work without salary to help in education radio venture to reach out to 90 Eskimo villages. Radio experience, excellent references, auditions tape, and photo to Father Jim Poole, Box 988, Nome, Alaska, 99762." It is pleasant to be able to note in passing that over the years Father Jim has been singularly blessed in the quality of volunteers he has been able to attract to his cause.

Nurse Ida Schilter's year in Nome ended the month after KNOM signed on. That she had donated her total year's earnings to the station was, of course, much appreciated. "But, I think," wrote Father Jim in the August *Static*, "the best gift she has given us all year is her spirit of generosity and charity toward all of us here at KNOM." Ida's Nome year had an exceptionally happy ending, for she flew south to "wedding bells with a great guy." That great guy was Tom Karlin, one of her co-volunteers at KNOM.

Over the years numerous ex-volunteers have married fellow ex-volunteers, or found a spouse in Nome. Many former KNOM volunteers — some married, some not — have made Nometown hometown. The "Old Fogey Night" held several times a year usually draws around 25 ex-KNOM volunteers.

Other staff changes were taking place about this time. Carol Razewski came from Schenectady, New York, to take over secretarial duties. Helen Osdieck — soon appreciated for her vim and vigor, as well as her great sense of humor and generous spirit — came from St. Louis to fill the nursing slot vacated by Ida. From Eatonville, Washington, came Ida's sister, Lucy, to help with the cooking. Fred Dyen from Spokane replaced maintenance man Jack Carr. Don Pike, who had run a very "with it" show over in Korea, came from California to join the on-the-air crew. And from Nome itself came three young Eskimo volunteers: Dennis Pikonganna, Pat Taxac, and her sister Mildred, better known as "Blu." This trio was especially helpful when it came to creating educational spots calling for Eskimo voices.

Transmission 13

Hand-to-Mouth: 1971d

Two months after KNOM started broadcasting, it had concrete feedback — listener reports from 93 villages — that the people of the target area were picking up the station, were listening. Along with those of other villages, the villagers of places like Tuntutuliak, Toksook Bay, Chuathbaluk, Eek were tuned in, turned on, enjoying the

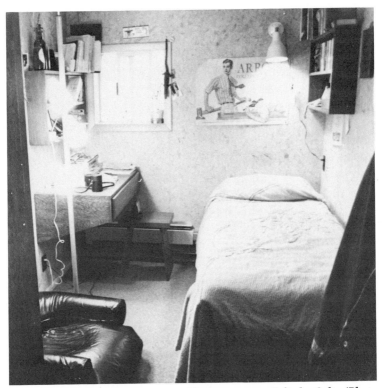

A volunteer's typical dorm room. Most rooms are 6 ft. by 9 ft. *(Photo by Tom Busch)*

many hours of airborne inspiration, education, and entertainment promised them when the station first went on the air.

Thanks to KNOM's far-reaching, reassuring voice the transistorized berry-picker, the solitary reindeer herder out on the tundra, the family at the fish camp now found themselves less alone, the bite of the mosquito less vicious, the work less tedious. Soon the trapper checking his line, and the patient fisherfolk hooking for tomcod through holes in the Bering Sea ice, too, would be warmed and cheered by KNOM's presence. Many such listeners wrote KNOM, and the incoming fan mail did much to boost the morale of the young deejays.

Honeymoon euphoria was still running high at KNOM as the third month of broadcasting came to an end. "I am more than happy;" wrote Father Jim in the October 1971 *Static*, "I'm on cloud nine!" Nevertheless, there were sobering, almost daily reminders that it was still a struggle to carry on, that every month had to be "sweated out." Now the Chevy was getting down to the "just barely running stage." An appeal went out to friends for Betty Crocker coupons for a new van. A pile came in, but never enough for the hoped-for van.

The KNOM staff at this time numbered 17. While all, except Father Jim, were volunteers, they still needed to be flown in and out, housed and fed. Those who stayed on for additional years were given an annual vacation trip out and back. "It's one of those 'absolutes,'" wrote Father Jim, "when you speak of mental health up here in the North, to get out of here for a vacation at least once a year."

One would not think that in the largest and least populated state in the union claustrophobia would be one of the major causes for concern. But such is the case, also at KNOM. The Nome area weather — with its frequent winds, rains, fogs, blizzards — tends to create an atmosphere of confinement, both physical and psychological. And the KNOM living conditions, too, are crowded, confining. The volunteers all do have their own rooms, but these are small, 6 x 9-foot cubicles, simply furnished with built-in bunks and desks.

Food, no matter how obtained, is expensive in remote Nome — 2,300 miles from Seattle. The KNOM table fare, served buffet style, has never been lavish, but it has always been wholesome, well prepared, sufficient. The only items served sparingly are fresh fruits and vegetables, items prohibitively expensive in Nome. To compensate in part for the lack of these, the volunteers religiously chew their vitamin-C tablets — bottled winter sunshine.

As far as Father Jim is concerned, there is no compromising in the matter of food. Hard-working young people, living under spartan, stress conditions need and deserve, he insists, at least decent meals. Good food, good morale. Good morale, good radio — and a happy gang. Actually, in spite of being in a high-cost area, KNOM continues to feed its staff for an average of less than $2.75 per person per day. It is a tribute to KNOM's attempts at extreme thriftiness that the food cost per volunteer rose less than 20% in one decade.

Travel and food costs are only part of KNOM's over-all financial picture. There are — along with many and various other items — also the regular monthly water, telephone, A.P. Wire Service, and electric bills. A decade after going on the air, KNOM was paying almost $40,000 a year for electricity. According to a survey made by the Alaska Cooperative Extension Service, it costs 209% of the national average — over twice as much — to feed a family of four in Nome for one week. Most everything else is proportionately expensive. "How about that for a depressing thought for the day!" reflected Father Jim. But then, he knew from the outset that getting a radio station on the air and keeping it there would be "an uphill drag all the way."

About the only really modest expense KNOM has had over the years is the weekly allowance paid each volunteer.

The first ones received the lordly sum of $5.00. This has subsequently been raised several times because of inflation and to conform to regulations imposed by the Social Security System.

From month to month, the whole KNOM operation has been, according to Tom Busch, "a hand-to-mouth existence...Mostly we live from crisis to crisis." Only Father Jim's relentless begging in *Static* after *Static*, the donated nurses' salaries, and Tweet's careful monitoring of all money-related matters have kept crises from becoming disasters, have kept the station from fiscal ruination.

What really keeps KNOM going? What is its mainspring? Father Jim's answer: "She sits at the desk right at

Tweet Burik at her office desk, 1984. *(Photo by Tom Busch)*

the front door of KNOM — Tweet Burik, KNOM's Business Manager." Once he described Tweet as "actually the glue that holds the place together."

It has really been Tweet who has kept the books balanced, the food on the table, the station on the air — and the mud off the floor. "Wipe your feet!" "Take off your boots!" "Don't track in mud!" "Yes, Tweetie Bird!" — as she is sometimes called teasingly, but affectionately. In mudville Nome the battle goes on almost without interruption. Only the hard freeze and snows of winter put an end to it. This writer personally once counted no less than seven different doormats, carpets, boot-scrapers between the outer door and the lunch counter in the Green House (the rectory-kitchen-dining room wing of the church building, painted green on the outside).

Earlier there was mention of John Huck, the Jesuit brother who headed the band of itinerant construction workers that helped build the KNOM studio. "Everyone loved Huck deeply and without exception," wrote Tom Busch. "One evening, in the fall of 1971, I was on the board. Father Poole called with a news item. A volunteer from St. Marys, a Pilot Station man, and Huck had all been lost and presumed drowned along the Yukon River. They'd been hunting at Pilot and were returning to St. Marys when their small boat apparently capsized. Only debris was found. I told Father Poole it would take me a while to write the story. I put an album side on the air, laid my head on the console — and wept about half an hour." Brother Huck is officially listed as having died on 8 October 1971. He was 33 years old at the time. R.I.P.

Sometime in November support nurse Karen Zweiger from Oshkosh, Wisconsin, joined the staff. That same month father of the Early Bird Show Alex Hills — after establishing himself as one of KNOM's favorite announcers — finished his tour of volunteer duty and departed Nome to join RCA Alascom. He later went on to become Alaska's Deputy Commissioner of Administration, and the state's chief telecom-

The KNOM Christmas star. *(Photo by Jim Green)*

munications official. At this writing Dr. Hills is a professor at the University of Alaska-Fairbanks.

Concerning Alex — clearly a man with a sure instinct for the fitting and a perfect sense of timing, as well as a delightfully skewed sense of humor — Tom Busch wrote, referring to the time he, Tom, was working on the transmitter tower: "We'd been turning on the studio-transmitter microwave every day, and Alex at the studio would occasionally play music for our entertainment. My distinct memory of the operation is of leaning over backwards from the tower to tighten cable clamps, with the country songs 'Please Help Me, I'm Falling' and 'Timber!' blaring from a loudspeaker on the roof of the building 157 feet below. 'Some joke!' I told him later."

For Christmas 1971 Tom Busch and John Pfeifer mounted a great star, illuminated by multi-colored lights, on the 70-foot tower next to the studio "to shine forth to all the countryside." This star, known as "the KNOM Christmas Star" — now an annual feature of Christmas in Nome — recalls the golden cross of electric lights that crowned the steeple of old St. Joseph's Church and seemed to hang by an invisible thread in the dark arctic sky. This "white man's star," as the Eskimos called it, was visible for a distance of over 20 miles. It was illuminated each evening to serve as a beacon to many a weary miner or musher groping his way through the winter darkness or a blizzard. The KNOM Christmas star — along with the slender 236-foot KNOM transmitter tower three miles east of Nome — is, like Alaska's flag, a present-day "beacon bright," a symbol of joy and hope, dedicated to help people find the way.

KNOM spot: *If miracles happen in mid-air, exploding like fireworks in a dark sky, they seldom happen when we ask for them. But when people are hungry, sick, lonely or troubled, a person who cares and loves can work miracles.*

Transmission 14

Staff Benefits: 1972

Reflecting on the year just ended, Father Jim wrote in the January 1972 *Static*: "What a tremendous year this one has been! So many dreams come true, so many prayers answered! I would say that aside from the year I was ordained this has been the biggest year of my life. And, of course, I owe it all to you folks for making it come true. Your kindness, generosity, and sacrifice have turned what was once called 'an idle pipe dream' into a humming 10,000-watt radio station. I want to thank you very, very much for making all of those dreams a reality."

Father Jim is given the credit for getting KNOM on the air, and this he surely deserves. However, alone he could never have done it — and he is the one who will most insist on this. His gratitude to his benefactors is genuine and boundless, and in *Static* after *Static* he emphasizes this. Without their donated dollars — and without the competent, dedicated, faithful volunteers — KNOM would never have come about nor enjoyed the success that it has.

Father Jim knows full well also that unless the Lord, too, build the house, build the station, we humans build in vain. He sees KNOM as essentially a spiritual enterprise, a space age apostolic outreach — "the very unusual business of selling God on 780 kilocycles" — and so we find in almost every "Transmission" of the *Static* also repeated, urgent pleas for prayers: "Pray hard for us... I need your prayers to back this work, and I need them badly... Your contributions and prayers help us keep it all together."

Again, staff turnover. In early 1972 newsman Scott Diseth from Tacoma came to replace Alex Hills, and Mary

Eileen "Meg" Gabriel came from Philadelphia as a support nurse to replace Sally Duggan. Sally later married fellow ex-KNOM volunteer Jack Carr. Also, at about this time, Chuck Newberg arrived to take over the Evening Show from departing Leo Kehs. Nurse Kitty Orris — "very faithful, very generous" — was by this time no longer at KNOM. She was, however, still in Nome, working now as a traveling nurse for the Norton Sound Health Corporation.

A staff member with no intentions of rotating out was the host of the Saturday Afternoon Show, Father Jim himself. In letter after letter people kept asking him how he was doing as a disk jockey. His answer, "I think it would be best treated in silence." He did admit, however, that doing his show was no longer the traumatic experience it first was, and that he was getting less rusty as time went on, though he was still "running into all sorts of boo-boos."

This may come as somewhat of a surprise, but Tom Busch writes: "Some people just naturally feel comfortable on the radio and some people don't. Father Poole is one of the latter unfortunates. He is an outstanding speaker; he communicates well over radio as well as in person, but he just is not comfortable with the dials and knobs."

Busch went on to narrate the following Poole "boo-boo":

"First, you have to understand that in a studio, turning on a microphone ordinarily turns off, 'mutes,' that studio's speaker in order to prevent feedback. That's why announcers customarily wear headphones that are hooked into the air signal.

"Well, one day in 1972 I was over at the Green House listening to Father Jim's Saturday Request Show, when it suddenly sounded as though the station had gone off the air. We had had a lot of trouble with electric power and I was accustomed to jumping up from what I was doing and steaming out to the transmitter.

"But it sounded to me like a quiet carrier, like we were still on the air but without programming. And then I heard 'room noises' coming over the radio. And then the phone rang. I heard Father Poole's voice coming both over the phone and over the radio telling me we were off the air.

"I tried telling him that we WERE on the air, but he was so convinced we weren't that I ran over — to find his microphone on. He'd apparently leaned over when his mike was on and his headphones had come unplugged. So, there he was, dead headphones, quiet speaker, convinced he was off the air."

KNOM spot: *Have you ever noticed how seriously we take ourselves most of the time? Every little criticism is a real disaster! We should just learn to laugh at ourselves more. We would always have something to laugh at.*

By the time KNOM celebrated its first anniversary on the air, a fair number of personnel changes had taken place. Richard Gembler, a newsman with eight years of experience, arrived from Austin, Texas, on 21 March, the first day of spring — and minus 32 degrees! In the early summer Pia Thompson came from St. Marys to be the first full-time Eskimo to serve on the KNOM staff. Les Brown — a broadcast engineer on leave from WTEV-TV Providence, R.I. — his wife Paula, and their preschool son, Vincent, arrived from Swansea, Massachusetts, in July. They were the first married couple to serve at KNOM. Les was a radio announcer, Paula taught catechism. During that summer Chris Brockway helped out with maintenance and with the setting up of a garage-workshop building.

For some KNOMers the trail led south during the first part of 1972. After three years of "faithful and loving service" in Nome, catechist Sister Paula Cosko returned to Seattle. Don Pike, Karen Zweiger, Carol Razewski — "faithful and patient secretary" — and "Big John" Pfeifer also finished their tours of volunteer duty and took their leave. Carol and John also took one another, as partners in marriage. John is now News Director for KMXT-FM in Kodiak. It might be added here that leave-taking after a volunteer hitch at KNOM can be unbelievably difficult for some. When it came time for Carol to leave, she sneaked out of town a day before her announced departure, fearing she would not be able to handle the emotions of a farewell. About this same time KNOM's first News Director, Harry Gallagher, left. It was Harry who developed the term "update," which KNOM has used ever since. While at KNOM he won the award for the best radio documentary of the year in Alaska for his "Suicide Documentary." Harry went back into commercial television Outside. He wound up anchoring the evening news at Detroit's CBS TV affiliate. In 1982, in Detroit, Harry died of cancer. He was 44 years old. R.I.P.

In the July 1972 *Static* we read: "Stranded, but happy! Or you could call it the 'Sledge Island Adventure.'" In a Native skinboat a group of volunteers took off on a trip to that island 25 miles up the coast. The weather changed. They spent two days and two nights camping out on the beaches of the Bering Sea, catching fish and cooking them on an open fire. For days after they talked about their miscarried but thrilling outing.

While the KNOM volunteers are expected to carry out, faithfully and conscientiously, their basic assigned duties — and to lend a hand with chores and at times of special need — they are not slaves. After their day's work is done, they are free to spend the time as they wish. The same goes for their regular days off. The Sledge Island outing is but one example of the many outings and activities available to them.

Over the years volunteers have fished the rivers of the Nome area, hiked and camped in the hills and mountains north of Nome, hunted moose and ptarmigan, driven the roads out of Nome, entered the Nome River Raft Race, combed the Bering Sea coast, jigged for crab and tomcod through holes in the Bering Sea ice. Some of the more hardy have even taken a swim in its icy waters. The Memorial Day Swim is popular also with some of the volunteers. However, most find the baths at Pilgrim Hot Springs far more inviting and make them a regular excursion goal.

For the athletically inclined, Nome offers quite a variety of sports, both indoor and outdoor. Many volunteers have either played or coached sports such as basketball, softball, volleyball. Many have run in the Midnight Sun Marathon. Jogging is a year-round sport, as is swimming in Nome's indoor pool. Father Jim was a major promoter of the pool.

Popular winter sports include ice skating, cross-country skiing, sledding, dog mushing and racing. While not exactly a sport at subzero temperatures, KNOM's fire-on-the-ice picnics are, nevertheless, popular events. It is not surprising that at these the demand for hot chili, hot dogs, hot chocolate far exceeds that for cold macaroni salad. The volunteers are encouraged to get out, to be active, all the more so in winter when — owing to long nights, darkness, blizzards — the walls tend to close in, mild attacks of cabin fever to break out.

The area around Nome has enriched many a volunteer's rock, driftwood, wildflower specimen collections. Most all have picked uncountable berries, especially blueberries. Photo buffs have found a rich variety of motifs, including spectacular displays of the northern lights. Be your hobby chess, play acting, Native arts and crafts, Eskimo dancing, talent shows, Fourth of July parade marching, ham radio, Boy or Girl Scouting, it can be pursued in Nome. Many volunteers have continued their education or taken special courses at Nome's Northwest Community College.

Along with recreation outings, KNOM volunteers, as we have seen, frequently enjoy also business outings, trips in bush planes to western Alaska villages for news stories, for experience of village life, or for purposes of medical escort missions. Among the preferred business-pleasure trips have been those to Savoonga on St. Lawrence Island to cover the annual Walrus Carnival there. The most exciting, however, have been those trips connected with the coverage of the annual Iditarod Trail Sled Dog Race.

The very first volunteers to serve in Nome were already part of Nome community life; and over the years the volunteers have always been a major part of the Nome community. But from the beginning, too, one of Father Jim's chief, ongoing goals at KNOM has been "to create a loving Christian community where we can grow spiritually

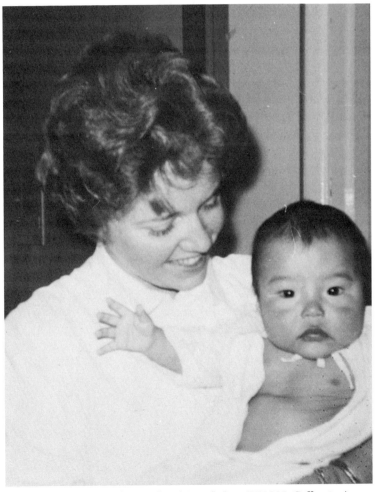

Nurse Penny Wicker and Eskimo baby. *(KNOM Collection)*

and reach out into our local community and touch the lives of others."

The kind of volunteer he looks for is one — to quote from his job description — "close to Faith, who wants to develop spiritual life, and interested in community living. Must have sense of humor." To develop spiritual life, there are at KNOM well prepared liturgies, prayer sessions, recollection days, retreats. Community spirit is fostered by various community activities such as birthday parties, potluck dinners, talent shows, hi-bye parties, group outings, gift exchanging at Christmas, and the like.

Les Brown taking his turn as dishwasher after the evening meal. *(KNOM Collection)*

KNOM spot: *I've turned off the motors, the TV, the radio. I've stopped my work and my play. I've stepped aside from my family and friends. I've even left planning and worrying for a few moments. I'm just listening, Lord. Speak to my heart.*

How successful has the KNOM community experiment been? Father Jim wrote of it: "What I really wish is that each of you could see this whole operation in person. The day by day operation of a large group of volunteers like this is something one has to participate in to really appreciate. It's a mixture of ideals, sharing, generosity, homesickness, good humor, gentleness, a touch of genius, cold noses and feet, surprises and remembered birthdays, and finally goodbyes and lifetime friends. It's an experience that you, a volunteer, or I myself, could never forget, would never want to forget. It's a rich life!"

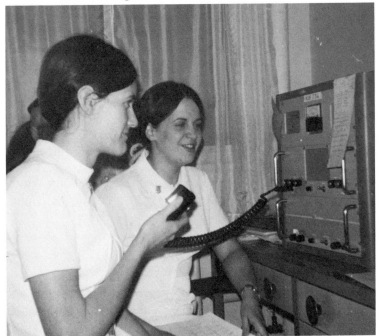

Candy Gleason, left, and Meg Gabriel talking on the radio with a village health aide. (Alaskan Shepherd *Collection*)

August 1972 brought with it yet more volunteer replacements. From Portland, Oregon, came nurse Candy Gleason, and from Indiana, nurse Penny Wicker. Jackie Singleton — soon dubbed "the professor" because of her glasses, her much reading, and her interest in botany — came from Colorado to work in the kitchen and as a part-time announcer. Jerry Springer came from Spokane to help put together generator buildings and install standby generators.

Soon after KNOM went on the air, it found itself plagued with power outages. Owing to outages, the station was off the air no less than 69 times during the first year of operation. Some of the outages lasted only a few seconds; the longest lasted 28 hours. "One of the saddest announcements you have to make on the air is 'KNOM is now going off the air,'" Father Jim wrote. He saw a solution to the problem only in KNOM's having its own standby generators. By September, Joe Miller — newly arrived from Santa Clara, California — Fred Dyen, Jerry Springer, and Les Brown, after working on many days up to midnight, finally had the two generators installed and working, one at the station and one at the transmitter site. Over the years these generators have rendered invaluable standby service. Thanks to them, and to automatic switchover equipment, power failures now take KNOM off the air for less than three seconds. The signal comes back automatically.

As the year 1972 was drawing to a close, Sheila Ames from Olympia, Washington, joined the nursing staff, and Jim Tighe from California the news staff.

Transmission 15

The Iditarod: 1973

In January 1973, with prospects of a radio job back home, Chuck Newberg said goodbye to KNOM and left to pursue elsewhere his radio career. This was to include, among other positions, that of City Clerk in Shishmaref. Over the years many former KNOM radio personalities — after having served a kind of internship at KNOM — have found futures in commercial radio. That same month "Smiling Lucy" Schilter returned to Nome for another year of volunteer service. The following month Pete Van Nort came from Sacramento to join the radio staff. He brought with

Jackie Singleton and Pete Van Nort. *(KNOM Collection)*

him such radio experience as he had gained from operating a pirate radio station in the basement of his Sacramento home. KNOM was his first real radio job. A year or two in Alaska, he thought, would about do it. It did not work out that way. He married Jackie Singleton and settled in Fairbanks, where he became the manager of radio station KIAK — and a decade later, President of Alaska Broadcasters Association. (It was in December 1984, during Pete's tenure as president of the A.B.A., that the F.C.C. elevated KNOM — along with a dozen other Alaskan stations — from a Class II station to a I-N station with extended long-distance protection. The drive for the action began during Tom Busch's presidency two years earlier.) Pete, according to Tom Busch, "brought tremendous creativity to KNOM's production. The KNOM 1974 Christmas play, 'A Christmas Carol' by Dickens, for which he was technical director, is a masterpiece."

In March head newsman Richard Gembler, KNOM's second News Director, left the station to go to work for radio KFAR in Fairbanks. Richard was the prime mover behind a number of KNOM projects, among them the upgrading of the production studio. It was under his initiative that KNOM brought up CBS Radio for an evening for the 1972 election night coverage.

Also in March three Nome Eskimo girls, junior volunteers Loretta Muktoyuk, Miki Sebwenna, and Marilyn Koezuna, worked at the station in housekeeping and record library positions. They were also a great help in making educational spots.

In April Scott Diseth finished his KNOM year and went on to work for KYAK in Anchorage, and then to become Program Director of KDLG in Dillingham, Alaska. During the month before his departure Scott won high praise for himself as a radio man, by doing a most commendable job as a ham radio operator when KNOM provided total coverage for the first annual 1,049-mile Anchorage to Nome Iditarod Trail Sled Dog Race.

A typical windswept winter day at the KNOM transmitter overlooking the Eskimo fish camp of Fort Davis and the frozen Bering Sea, 1980. *(KNOM Collection)*

For no other yearly event does the KNOM team pull together as totally and selflessly as it does for the Iditarod. On foot, by automobile, by snowmobile, in "the race plane," by two-way radio, by ham radio, by telephone, the team has for over a decade covered what is billed as "The Last Great Race" from its starting line in Anchorage to the finish line in Nome. The nurses included, all the staff — working "on the board," or scattered along the trail or in the air as spotters calling in daily, hourly reports on the progress of the mushers, or over on Front Street making finish-line broadcasts and interviewing arriving mushers — from the first-place winner to the last-place "Red Lantern" finisher — have shared in the excitement and fatigue of covering, around the clock, this, by now world famous, dog-mushing classic. The 1978 finish, when Dick Mackey won first place by one second — by the length of his lead dog — was an exceptionally exciting one for the KNOM gang. Mackey was one of the men who helped put up the KNOM antenna tower back in the construction days.

The KNOM transmitter tower and Dick are mutually indebted; a bond of genuine affection exists between the two. Whether Dick is traveling by dogteam or airplane, the tower is to him a "special welcome sight." This is particularly true when he rounds Cape Nome and comes down the homestretch of the Iditarod Trail. (Dick has plumbed the tower twice, without charge. In 1978 he found it 8″ off plumb at the top and slightly twisted, probably by stress from the 1974 storm, and by the 70+ MPH windstorm of December 1977 that destroyed the old KNOM Christmas star. In 1984 he found it only 3″ off plumb.)

Various stations, including the Armed Forces Radio Network, have come to rely on KNOM for Iditarod coverage. In 1980 the station's workload was eased considerably by a Code-A-Phone, courtesy of Sohio. This handled over 400 calls throughout the race. By 1984 no fewer than 26 stations in Canada and Alaska, including three in the city of Anchorage, were carrying KNOM's live coverage of the first Iditarod finisher.

In 1979 a special award was conferred by the International Sled Dog Racing Association on KNOM and Tom Busch for outstanding reporting of the Iditarod and cooperation with Outside media by sharing information gathered by KNOM. In 1984 KNOM won the Alaska Press Club's "First Place, Live Sports Broadcasts" honor for its coverage of the Iditarod. Proudly Tom Busch displays a silver tray he received from *Team and Trail* magazine for his Iditarod reporting.

KNOM spot: *The Iditarod Dog Sled Race from Anchorage to Nome means many risks for the mushers. They take risks for the adventure and personal satisfaction. Being a Christian is also a risky way of life. To be like Christ and follow Him, He asks us to make sacrifices. If we're willing to take risks for adventure and personal satisfaction, we should be willing to take the risk to follow Jesus totally. The reward is a lot greater.*

Tom Busch, left, and Richard Gembler appear on camera during the short-lived "Nome Evening Report" on Nome T.V. Cable. *(Photo by Tom Busch)*

In the May 1973 *Static* we read: "Forty months of distinguished service! That is the service record of Tom Busch, KNOM Chief Engineer, who was here to plan and lay out the whole station and has been keeping us on the air ever since, through some pretty troublesome and challenging electronic problems. Tom will be moving on to commercial radio as Chief Engineer at KIAK in Fairbanks. Tom has made a tremendous contribution to KNOM in his technical skill. But over and above that, the generous and friendly person that is Tom has made him a lifelong friend of all the staff and so many others here in Nome and in our listening audience." This appreciation by Father Jim.

By this time Busch was into his fourth year as a volunteer, and — to hear him tell it — "developing itchy feet." It was the 1973 Iditarod that, quite unexpectedly, occasioned a change in jobs for Tom.

"Bob Fleming," wrote Tom, "the owner of KYAK Anchorage, flew to Nome to anchor our simulcast finish-line coverage. The morning Dick Wilmarth, the winner, arrived, I was soldering connectors in the engineering room. I'd been up all night, thought I looked like hell, and no doubt was less than coherent. Bob dropped by and we started talking, about radio, about nothing in particular. Just offhand I asked if he had any engineering positions open.

"'I sure do, and you've got it!' came the unexpected reply. Turns out that one reason for his Nome trip was to recruit personnel for his new station in Fairbanks, KIAK. In late May I was off to Fairbanks for two glamorous years."

Tom was "perfectly content" at KIAK, and the last thing on his mind was to return to KNOM. But, stay tuned for more about the Busch-KNOM connection!

Comings and goings are as normal a part of KNOM life as are inhaling and exhaling. Given the nature of volunteer staffing, it can hardly be otherwise. Smiles and tears on the tarmac are routine. And yet, for all that, they are always sincere and fresh, as volunteer after volunteer

Aerial view of Nome, looking west, May 1973. (*Photo by Tom Busch*)

Nome, 1973. The KNOM-St. Joseph's Church compound is visible toward the lower left corner of the picture. (*Photo by Tom Busch*)

comes and goes, cracks a smile and sheds a tear. It is nothing short of amazing how quickly new volunteers become so integral a part of the close-knit KNOM family that, when departure time comes, the leave-taking is truly heartwrenching for some.

"We will all miss her a great deal," wrote Father Jim in that same May 1973 *Static* of Penny Wicker. "Penny has cheerfully helped out in so many ways besides nursing." According to Tom Busch, "Penny, despite stiff competition, is the undisputed all-time pun champion of the volunteer dinner table."

By the end of May, Roy Wells had flown up from Las Cruces, New Mexico, in his Ercoupe to be Chief Engineer. Along with his considerable technical skills, he brought with him an engaging sense of humor. Also, by the end of May, Helen Osdieck was welcomed back for another year of KNOM-Nome nursing.

During the summer, the Browns finished their year and departed. Les is remembered for his prowess in helping scrounge oil tanks found out on the tundra or at abandoned mining camps. He left an account of an oil tank scrounging excursion he made up the Kougarok Road with Fred Dyen and Jerry Springer.

"Again we had the rented flatbed, the KNOM Chevy Suburban, and this time a full welding rig, along with a 50-gallon drum of gas for the trucks.

"First off, on arrival, we threw the gas drum off the flatbed and rolled it around and fueled both trucks. We didn't notice that the drum had leaked as we rolled it, and we had made a complete circle around the trucks.

"There were three tanks made from sections of pipe with ends welded in, each three feet in diameter and about 24 feet long. We manhandled two of them up onto the flatbed, though they stuck off the back quite a distance. For the third one we cut up a long abandoned truck and fashioned a sort of trailer by chaining the truck parts directly onto the pipe section. But that was where the trouble began.

When we started to cut, sparks from the torch ignited the ring of gasoline we had unknowingly made around the trucks. Worse, the oxygen tank was sitting inside the ring. There were a few panicky moments as we beat the fire out with our jackets.

"Ultimately, we *did* get everything loaded and set out for Nome. I rode the flatbed with Jerry. The Kougarok Road is up and down some good-sized hills with lots of

Jeanne Gabriel, 1974, "crabbing" through a hole in the Bering Sea ice. *(KNOM Collection)*

hairpin turns. Naturally it's all gravel, and rough gravel at that. We had the truck loaded so badly with pipe sticking off the rear that it would tip up off the front wheels if you went over any large rock. This was a little upsetting when it happened on a curve, since it was then impossible to steer for a few seconds. The trip took several hours, and we really weren't done until well after midnight."

Les Brown is remembered, too, for spending long hours designing and installing the electrical system of the standby generators. At KNOM he did the Evening Show, and later became News Director. His wife Paula, C.C.D. (Confraternity of Christian Doctrine) teacher, was replaced by new arrival Jeanne Gabriel, Meg's sister.

Maintenance man, electrician, diesel mechanic, welder, and fixer of just about anything — "most of all a nice guy" — Joe Miller left at this time, intent upon a career in law. Lucy Schilter — "really appreciated for all her great qualities" — too, left at this time. Jerry Springer returned to do more maintenance work. From Puyallup, Washington, came Kathy Zasimovich to do secretarial work, and from New Orleans newscaster Mike Dorner. Joining the staff about this time, from Philadelphia, was Kate Lawless — "a pretty, young registered nurse, very gentle in manner, with a name that brings her a bit of teasing."

Enter the Paulists! Wrote Father Jim in the July 1973 *Static*: "Four very wonderful summer additions to our staff from the Paulist Fathers. Fr. George Fitzgerald, and seminarians Jim Illig, Jack Ryan, and Jerry Bier have been a real morale boost to our gang and a tremendous help in the work here. Fr. George replaced me while I was absent. Jim has operated a 'Walk-In Center' for problems in drinking and drugs, and has worked with alcohol rehabilitation. He has also done a lot of work in radio and educational spots. Jack has worked at the hospital and the Teen Center, and has helped out with the radio spots and sermons. Jerry has worked regularly at the Teen Center, started a Little League program, given guitar lessons to teenagers, worked in radio talks and spots, and helped out with our liturgies and even preached at the Methodist Church. All of them have been simply great, and the Paulists are definitely down as wanted men in Nome!"

From the time Father Jim first thought about radio for western Alaska, he saw the urgent need for having programming in the different Eskimo languages of that region. First steps in this direction were taken in the summer of 1973, when educational spots in Central Yup'ik, Siberian Yup'ik, and Inupiaq were produced. Producing spots in these languages was not easy, for the person producing a given spot had to know both English and the Eskimo in question very well. This same summer also a daily program of important news of the day was initiated in Central Yup'ik. Registered nurse Rose Beans Towarak and certified teacher Cecilia Ulroan, both St. Marys grads and good friends of Father Jim, made this possible. Marilyn Koezuna was at this time doing headlines in Inupiaq.

During the last months of 1973, yet more personnel changes took place. From Eau Claire, Wisconsin, came nurse Bonnie Reilly to join the support staff. She replaced the "very faithful" Candy Gleason, who went on to work for the Norton Sound Health Corporation. Meg Gabriel — known for her generous spirit and caring smile — finished a double tour of KNOM-Nome nursing duty and moved on to a nursing position in Kotzebue. It will be remembered that Meg has since become Mrs. Alex Hills. Sheila Ames, too, finished her year and departed — along with her sister, Cathy, who had spent the summer at KNOM in a support position. Sheila was to be "missed a great deal by the whole gang." Steve Havilland came from Washington, D.C., to be News Director. Nomeites Roy Silvernail joined the staff as an announcer, and Karen Nagozruk began a three-year stint of "loving service" as record librarian and office worker.

KNOM spot: *Fishing and hunting takes lots of patience. Sometimes, just when we're ready to give up and move on, that herd of walrus or school of salmon is spotted. It makes the waiting worthwhile. People require our patience, too. Wouldn't it be nice if we could have as much patience with the people we know as when we're hunting and fishing? The reward is much greater, too.*

Transmission 16

Father Jim, Globetrotter: 1974

It took the first day of April, and some duplicity on the part of Roy Wells, to get Tweet to go on the air. She did have a license, but she had sworn she would never go on the air. On 1 April 1974 Roy asked her to just watch the board for a few minutes. She agreed. Ten minutes later, 20 minutes later, and still no Roy. Thus it was brought about that Tweet did her first show. It must not have been too traumatic an experience, for she agreed to do an hour-long show each day for the next several weeks.

Nurse Susan Dusenbury preparing dinner for the KNOM gang. *(KNOM Collection)*

Film maker and radio man Ed Guiragos came from New York in May to serve as an announcer. At the same time came three Paulist seminarians, Jack Lord, Mike Martin, and Terry Ryan, and the layman Richard Fleischmann for a summer of volunteer work. Stan Weisbeck came from Spokane in June to help man the board. Also in June, from Stockton, California, came Mary McGurk to work in the kitchen, and from Cleveland Father Joseph Henninger, S.J., to replace Father Jim for a few weeks. About this time nurse Helen Osdieck and Jackie Singleton, cook and weather girl, left, as did Roy Silvernail. Roy went on to do radio work for Uncle Sam in the Army.

Nurses Susan Dusenbury from San Leandro, California, and Colleen Marilley from Seattle came in July, the month Pete Van Nort left. Meanwhile Father Jim was on a 37-day, all expenses paid trip to Europe and Kenya, Africa — everything courtesy of Stanley Githunguri of Kenya, whom Father Jim had helped through his high school years while he was a student at St. Marys.

To celebrate its third anniversary on the air, KNOM decided to increase its hours of broadcasting by two, signing on at 6:00 A.M. and off at midnight. The new schedule went into effect on 1 August.

In August Jim Tighe left KNOM, but stayed on in Nome for a while, before going on to join station KSKA in Anchorage, and then stations in northern California. It was Jim who added a delightful touch of whimsy to KNOM's character, when he, to prove one of his spots true — that one can grill a cheese sandwich with an electric iron — gave a live demonstration outside the studio. He later married KNOM ex-volunteer Pat Wygant.

That same August Lou Ann Diamond arrived from N. Attleboro, Massachusetts, to help Tweet with the office work, and Mark Hoelsken came from Denver to serve as an announcer and chief engineer.

September, too, saw staff changes. New to KNOM-Nome were newsman Gene Kane from St. Ann, Missouri, short-term radio engineer Mike Rizzone from Dallas, maintenance man Mike West from Houston, and nurses Pat Wygant from Olympia Fields, Illinois, and Romey DeFuria from Seattle. During the summer Michael McGilney and Greg Molica helped out as announcers.

On 11 November 1974 a storm so severe and damaging hit Nome that President Gerald Ford declared the city and western Alaska a disaster area. City power, lights, water, phones were knocked out. The airport was shut down. King

Tom Busch interviewing Jim Tighe as the latter, to prove one of his spots true — that one can grill a cheese sandwich with an electric iron — gives a live demonstration outside the studio, 1972. *(KNOM Collection)*

Island village on the east end of Nome was totally leveled. KNOM itself survived the hurricane-force winds and the high, raging surf. Its towers were left standing, its generators still operative. For almost 24 hours it and KICY were the only means of getting news out of the stricken city.

Steve Havilland, though a hunt-and-peck typist, distinguished himself, nevertheless, as he stuck to a manual keyboard and tapped messages out to the rest of the world. For several days all at the station worked around the clock, helping with the distribution of food and clothing. KNOM stayed on the air for 42 consecutive hours, handling emergency messages and relaying Civil Defense announcements to the people of Nome and western Alaska. It was "a mighty dazed looking crew when things finally quieted down," wrote Father Jim. In recognition of Steve's work during the time of the storm, KNOM received an Associated Press Citation for "outstanding achievements in cooperative news coverage." Over the years KNOM staff members have had a great number of their stories accepted by the A.P. News Service.

KNOM spot: *When life becomes a grind, remember it's merely a test to see if you'll come out broken or polished.*

In December moist-eyed goodbyes again were said as the very popular Jeanne Gabriel, C.C.D. teacher and "helper in a thousand ways," faithful Kate Lawless, and Steve Havilland became "former volunteers" — but only for a time. All three were to return for yet another year of service at KNOM.

Joining the KNOM family at this time were radio man Dennis Principe from Parma Heights, Ohio, and C.C.D. teacher and nurse Gail Renshaw from Lansdale, Pennsylvania. These additions to Father Jim's "one great crew" were soon joined by two more: Mary Jones — "a very charming young Eskimo woman from Chevak" — who came to do translations into Central Yup'ik and to broad-

cast news in that language; and Mark Frankinberger —
a radio novice, but a social anthropologist specializing in
Eskimology — who came to be an announcer.

Transmission 17

Father Jim and Mother Teresa: 1975

"So fast fly the years," wrote Father Jim in the July 1975 *Nome Static*, "when they are filled with happiness and excitement and challenge. It seems but seven or eight months ago that we stood nervously poised over the control panel

KNOM and St. Joseph's Staff 1975-1976. (Left to Right) First Row: Colleen Marilley, R.N., Kate Lawless, R.N., Fr. Jim Poole, S.J., Florence Francis, Jeanne Gabriel; Second Row: Jay Lyman, Susan Dusenbury, R.N., Mark Hoelsken, Sue Hill, R.N., Steve Havilland; Third Row: Cathy Glidden, R.N., Bonnie Reilly, R.N., Mary Adams, R.N., Therese "Tweet" Burik, Tom Busch; Fourth Row: Greg Mitchell, Rick Barton, Bro. Normand Berger, F.I.C., Bro. Albert Heinrich, F.I.C. *(KNOM Collection)*

awaiting the Bishop's touch to send KNOM's first program out on the airways. But four years have actually passed — 1,460 days, 24,000 hours of broadcasting. We have learned a lot, much of it the hard way, but we have lived a lot too; and they have been good years.

"When July 14th rolled around and we aired our 'anniversary program,' the bits and pieces from our original first program did sound a little 'historical'; but they awakened a lot of beautiful memories also.

"Three thoughts always come to my mind on KNOM's birthdays. First, God has been so good to us. Secondly, all the wonderful, generous people who worked here during the building and then the operation of KNOM. Thirdly, all of the generous and loving people like yourselves who have been the lifeline to keep us going."

By July 1975 personnel changes had again taken place. Mary McGurk, who had cheered the gang with her fine cooking and pleasant disposition, left in May. Lou Ann Diamond — forever teased "Diamond Lou" — soon followed her.

In August yet more changes: "Wow," wrote Father Jim, "the comings and goings are enough to keep anyone on their toes. We said goodbye to radio people: Dennis Principe, Gene Kane, Stan Weisbeck, Marilyn Koezuna; nurses: Pat Wygant, Romey DeFuria (who married Dennis Principe); Paulist seminarians: John Cheviot and Chuck Kullman; and our man of all trades, Mike West. I can't really express how grateful I am for the generous and unselfish year they have given here at KNOM, but I know my prayers will follow each one of them wherever they go. Coming off the Wien jet these last few days were new maintenance man Jay Lyman from Colville, Washington, Rick Barton, D.J., from Pennsylvania, and Suzanne Hill, nurse, from Ohio. Expected in the next week or so are Catherine Glidden, nurse, from Oregon; Mary Adams, nurse, from Canada; Brother Normand Berger and Brother Albert Heinrich, radiomen, from Ohio. Both are members of the Brothers of Christian Instruction." Mary Nanuwak, a Registered Nurse from Chevak, Alaska, served as a short-term afternoon deejay in 1975.

In September nurse Cathy Glidden arrived from Portland, and Florence Francis came from St. Marys to work as an Eskimo translator, secretary, and deejay. Kate Lawless and

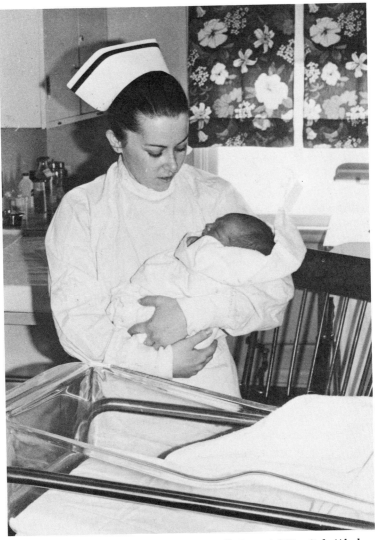

Mary Adams on duty at Maynard McDougall Memorial Hospital. (Alaskan Shepherd *Collection*)

Bonnie Reilly both returned for another year as support nurses. The following month they were joined by radio announcer Greg Mitchell from Bremerton, Washington. Before the year was out, Mary Adams arrived from Canada to round out the nursing staff. Mary has the distinction of being the only non-US citizen to serve at KNOM. Ed Guiragos left the station, but went on to make a film of the missions of northern Alaska for the Diocese of Fairbanks. He still recalls his time at KNOM "with extreme fondness and nostalgia." Gail Renshaw, too, left at this time, leaving behind her "many friends who won't soon forget her."

By now it should be obvious even to the casual reader that the KNOM/Father Jim Poole story is also a story of almost continuous staff turnover. Since the station is forced to depend almost entirely on volunteer staffing for its operation, it could hardly be otherwise. However, were it not for volunteers, past and present, there simply would never have been, there simply would not continue to be a KNOM. All along the KNOM staff has been, and continues to be, a synergistic entity, a complex mosaic composed mostly of many diverse, colorful, discrete elements — read *volunteers*, over 200 of them! KNOM is a reality far greater than the sum of its constituent parts.

From the outset Bishop Gleeson made it very clear that the station would have to see to its own financing and staffing, for the 409,849-square mile Diocese of Fairbanks, with only 14,000 Catholics, was a poor diocese, and he a poor bishop, a beggar bishop, who could do little toward the support of the station. Although the diocese's financial picture has brightened some during the last two decades, it still remains basically the same.

Nevertheless, as the KNOM years ticked off, it became more and more evident that something had to be done to insure greater basic staff stability and continuity. It was just too time and energy consuming for Father Jim to have to be forever recruiting and breaking in new people, forever worrying about qualified personnel at all levels of the operation. Bishop Whelan agreed. Accordingly, in the spring of 1975 something was done.

"Thank heavens! 'Uncle Tommy' Busch, KNOM's first engineer and planner of our radio setup, will be returning to KNOM," wrote Father Jim in May. As early as March 1971 he had expressed his hope concerning Tom's work at KNOM, "Who knows, maybe he'll make it a life's work." Now, just two years after Tom left KNOM, he was back, this time not as a volunteer, but as the very modestly salaried General Manager.

Tweet, the official Business Manager of the station, too, was by now receiving a salary, but so token — in keeping with her wishes — that her status was still virtually that of a volunteer. So modest were Tom and Tweet's salaries that the station continued to provide them with room and board. For well over a decade Father Jim, Tweet, and Tom were KNOM's core of stability and continuity.

KNOM's constant staff turnover should not be viewed as a negative feature about the station. Ever new personnel means ever new blood, new ideas, a built-in openmindedness. In many ways the whole radio venture has actually profited from its volunteer staffing nature. Hardly a volunteer has come and gone without effecting some change, one way or another, major or minor, for the better.

Regarding his own role at the station, Father Jim wrote as early as 14 December 1970 to his General Superior Father Bernard F. McMeel, "I will need another priest here within this next year or two who is very much interested in the radio apostolate and the idea of educational radio, someone who would gradually pick up the reins here as age and years catch up with me." All along Father Jim was convinced that the station should not "hinge on one person."

In Father Harold Greif Nome had a second priest and Father Jim a most devoted co-pastor — or "com-padre," as he dubbed him. But Father Greif was not into radio, and he spent much of his time home visiting and away from Nome caring for the people of Teller, Wales, and

Little Diomede. Fifteen years after Father Jim wrote the above, he was still the sole radio priest in Nome.

To help guarantee a future for KNOM, Father Jim felt the station needed — in addition to a second radio priest — also an endowment. About this he wrote to Bishop Gleeson way back on 9 January 1965, "It would be a fond dream that once the radio station is completed that the job of raising funds might continue, to set up an endowment fund, the interest of which would one day insure the financial success and permanency of the station." Over the years his constant begging has served only to keep the books balanced, albeit precariously. Twenty years after his letter to Bishop Gleeson a meaningful endowment fund is slowly becoming a dream realized.

You would think that, given KNOM's touch-and-go financial status, begging for the needs of the station would satisfy Father Jim's money-raising urges. Not so. Before 1975 was out, moved by the desperate plight of the poor served by Mother Teresa and her Missionaries of Charity, that inveterate beggar took it upon himself to collect funds on their behalf through the "Transmissions" of the *Static*, in St. Joseph's Church, and even from his volunteers. To his gratification, these latter, whose weekly allowance had by now been raised to $7.50, generously stuffed donations into the jar marked: "Mother Teresa — to feed the hungry of India."

The following year, in the Bronx, New York, Father Jim met her in person. "I know," he wrote, "it sounds strange to be begging for other causes when we have a cause of our own to support, prices rising, etc. But God takes care, and the needs of so many millions are so much more a matter of life and death than ours."

KNOM spot: *When we see the lilies of the field spinning in distress, worried how to create beauty; when we see all the birds building barns to store, then it will be time to worry. Until then, trust Him.*

Transmission 18

More Staff Rotation: 1976-77

Predictably, the summer of 1976 also saw considerable staff turnover. "Hurting hearts!" wrote Father Jim in the July *Static*. "No matter how light we make of it, the departure of our volunteers each year is really hard. Sue Dusenbury and Colleen Marilley, who have served faithfully for two years here at KNOM — Colleen two years as a support nurse and Sue one year as a nurse and one year as a 'super cook' — will be hard acts to follow. Florence Francis, secretary and D.J., young lady from St. Marys whom I have known since she was seven years old, will also be leaving. It's not easy to thank these volunteers just for their regular jobs, but how do you thank them for the million extra things they have done to make community life beautiful? We will miss them very much, but hope to see them again."

Though living in Seattle now, Colleen Marilley continues to be heard over KNOM as the voice introducing Morning Prayers and Father Jim's Inspirational Talks, each twice daily. She was also the voice introducing and closing out KNOM Encyclopedia, which was taken off the air on its ninth birthday, in November 1984. For all of this, Colleen is second only to Father Jim as the person most heard over KNOM, with something like 50,000 airings of her voice *after* her departure. And there will be more in the future, at least six a day. It goes without saying that Colleen is gifted with an unusually soft, clear, pleasant radio voice. "I used to tell her," wrote Tom Busch, "she was wasting her life as a nurse, saving lives and healing the sick when she could have a great future spinning hits."

Florence Francis both Father Jim and Tom Busch were to

see again. Stay tuned! Early morning disk jockey — and "a very nice guy and a dear friend" — Rick Barton, also departed about this time. Concerning him, Tom Busch said, "Rick arrived on a morning flight and was deejaying at 2 P.M. like he'd been doing it all his life. A popular feature of Rick's Morning Show was the 'Coffee Cup Toast,' when he'd invite listeners to toast the subjects of various kicker stories each morning."

By the end of August, after eleven new volunteers from

KNOM and St. Joseph's Staff 1976-1977. (Left to Right) First Row: Bro. Albert Heinrich, F.I.C., Claudia Butler, Mary Pat McElligott; Second Row: Coco Denegri, Steve Havilland, Fr. Jim Poole, S.J., Therese "Tweet" Burik; Third Row: Mary Nanuwak, Mary Ann Zellner, R.N., Chuck Tranfo, Karen Wickman, R.N., Jane Schraufnagel, R.N., Judy Hylton, Joanne Cagney, R.N.; Fourth Row: Luella "Mom" Poole, Tom Busch, Bro. Normand Berger, F.I.C., Joe Thompson, Rae Jean Blaschka, R.N., and Pat Lippert. *(KNOM Collection)*

all over the country had jet lagged into Nome, the staff was again up to full strength. New staff members were the following: Mary Pat McElligott, secretary and announcer, from Ione, Oregon; Claudia Butler, cook, from Long Beach, California; Judy Hylton, liturgist and teacher, from Oregon City, Oregon; Joe Thompson, maintenance, from Colfax, Washington; Karen Wickman, nurse, from Milwaukee; Joanne Cagney, nurse, from Ridgewood, New Jersey; Chuck Tranfo, radio announcer, from New Brunswick, New Jersey; Pat Lippert, radio announcer, from Portland, Oregon; Rae Jean Blaschka, nurse, from Camus, Washington; Jane Schraufnagel, nurse, from Leroy, Wisconsin; and Mary Ann Zellner, nurse, from Wilmette, Illinois. Jeanne Gabriel and Steve Havilland were back for yet another year at KNOM, as was Kate Lawless. Jesuit seminarian Tim Kaufmann

On a recreational outing and sitting on gold dredge buckets (From Left to Right): Coco Denegri, Father Jim, Claudia Butler, Joanne Cagney, and Brother Albert Heinrich, F.I.C. (Alaskan Shepherd *Collection*)

helped out during the summer. Tim had been a deejay at the most listened to radio station in the country, WABC New York, while still a teenager. He gave KNOM the news theme which the station continues to use. Originally produced for CKLW in Windsor, Ontario, the theme was given to KNOM by the vice-president of the production company which recorded it.

In September chief engineer Mark Hoelsken and maintenance man Jay Lyman boarded the jet and headed south. Jay later married Colleen Marilley.

Before 1976 ended, the jet trail led south for yet five

KNOM and St. Joseph's Staff 1977-1978. (Left to Right) First Row on stairs: Holly Nelson, R.N., Bro. Albert Heinrich, F.I.C., Timaree Bierle, R.N.; Second Row: Tweet Burik, Sue Boyle, Fr. Jim Poole, S.J.; Third Row: Chuck Tranfo, Zita Schiffelbein, R.N.; Fourth Row: Fr. Harold Greif, S.J., Bro. Norm Berger, F.I.C.; Fifth Row: Mary Pat McElligott, Colleen Harrington, Trese Ptaszynski, R.N., Annie Diffenbaugh, R.N.; Sixth Row: Tom Busch, Mark Hoelsken, Dr. Herbert Merz; On the Balcony: Chris Robling, Al Levitre, Pete Fricilone, Dr. Terry McMahon, Joanne Ambrosi, Ann Knobbe, R.N., Cary Bolling. *(KNOM Collection)*

more volunteers: Jeanne Gabriel, Cathy Glidden, Bonnie Reilly, and Greg Mitchell. "All," according to Father Jim, "put in a lot of love and care into their work and into the KNOM community." Jeanne was long remembered for her extraordinarily popular deejay program, for her "happy, happy, happy!" catch phrase.

Mid-1977 likewise saw the annual ritual of the changing of the KNOM guard. Departing were Jane Schraufnagel — "a marvelously loving and caring person in our community" — "dedicated nurse" Rae Jean Blaschka, "magnificent cook" Claudia Butler, and "generous support nurse" Mary Ann Zellner. Along with them exited also Karen Wickman — "a very faithful support nurse, who brightened the lives of the staff with her good humor and caring" — Joanne Cagney — "a real community support as well as a constant source of energetic enthusiasm" — and Coco Denegri — "a very lively member of the KNOM community and wonderfully helpful both as a D.J. and in the studio office."

Steve Havilland finished his 36th month at the station, where he "added a very professional touch to KNOM's news." Joe Thompson, who had kept the buildings intact, the motors running, the lights on — "but most of all he, in his quiet, loving way touched the lives of all at KNOM" — also left about this time. Morning man Pat Lippert went off to join the Jesuits. Over the years a number of ex-KNOM volunteers have become sisters and priests.

To replace departed veterans came newcomers: secretary Joanne Ambrosi from Gardena, California; nurse Ann Knobbe from St. Louis; cook Colleen Harrington from Seaside, Oregon; nurse Ann Diffenbaugh from Glen View, Illinois; maintenance man Peter Fricilone from Chicago; radio man Cary Bolling from Mobile, Alabama; nurse Trese Ptaszynski from Hartford, Connecticut; radio announcer Chris Robling from Washington, D.C.; nurse Zita Schiffelbein from Yakima, Washington; nurse Holly Nelson from Erie, Pennsylvania; and C.C.D. teacher and newsperson Sue Boyle from Chicago. Mark Hoelsken came back for a third year. The above were joined just before year's end by nurse Timaree Bierle from St. Louis.

The 3rd of September 1977 was a big day in the life

Wedding day, St. Marys Mission Chapel, 3 September 1977: Tom Busch, Florence Francis Busch, Father Jim. *(Photo by Brother Albert Heinrich, F.I.C.)*

of the KNOM family as the paths of yet two more KNOMers led to the altar. On that day Thomas Anthony Busch and Florence Margaret Francis took one another as husband and wife. The wedding took place at St. Marys, the bride's hometown. There to take part in the ceremonies and celebrations, both sacred and social, were four area priests, Bishop Whelan, and, of course, Father Jim. About ten people chartered from Nome to take part in the wedding rite and reception. This Nome group included Tom's mother and two aunts from the Philadelphia area — his entire close family. According to the groom, "It was really something!"

KNOM spot: *A wise lover values not so much the gift of the lover as the love of the giver.*

Transmission 19

Father Jim Makes *People Weekly:*

1978-79

Early in 1978 KNOM General Manager Tom Busch —
ever appreciative of Tweet Burik's contribution to the whole
KNOM operation — took it upon himself to make up and
send to Bella Hammond, wife of Alaska's Governor Jay

Chris Robling and Brother Albert Henirich, F.I.C., interviewing one-
time governor of Alaska, Walter Hickel, in Studio C. *(KNOM Collection)*

Hammond, a portfolio on Tweet. Some weeks later word reached Nome that Tweet was among those chosen for the "First Lady's Volunteer Award — 1979." From Mrs. Hammond she received a plaque as concrete evidence of the award. Tweet was at the time in her 14th year of volunteer work in Alaska.

Dr. Michael McMahon from La Jolla, California, arrived in Nome in April. He came as a volunteer support doctor to work in the new Norton Sound Regional Hospital. His donated salaries were a major shot in KNOM's financial arm. During the years 1977-79 the "delightful" Dr. Herbert Merz also did part-time support volunteer service.

How to celebrate KNOM's seventh birthday, Tom Busch wondered. By 1978 technology and the station's budget had advanced to the point where KNOM could think about doing something rather different, something adventurous. Tom got an idea: How about a broadcast from the top of Sledge Island! Now that would really be something different, and something sure to get and hold audience attention.

Sledge Island, 25 miles west of Nome, has long been a source of fascination to many Nomeites. There is something mirage-like, something mysterious about it. When Bering Sea light conditions are right, and swirling fogs enshroud it, the island seems to come alive, to move, to take on weird, grotesque shapes.

It was arranged to have King Islander Dean Pushruk take Mark Hoelsken, Joanne Ambrosi, and Colleen Harrington over to Sledge Island in his boat. Several times while en route, Mark "broke radio silence," with a few brief live reports from the boat. The party's destination was being kept a secret. Listeners were told only that KNOM on that 14 July would do a very unusual broadcast. From background noises, however, it was obvious that the party was traveling in a boat.

After around 80 pounds of equipment had been carried up the rocky slope to the plateau on top of the island,

Mark began the anniversary broadcast with, "This is Mark Hoelsken. I am talking to you from the top of Sledge Island. It is absolutely beautiful up here." Loud and clear his voice came over the waters, over the air.

Mark had two-way communications with Tom Busch, the anchorman back at the studio. Over the two-way Tom would transmit song titles, dictate messages and important announcements to Mark and his companions, and spin the records and play the spots. On the island Mark would then introduce the songs and broadcast the messages and make the announcements in such a way that the broadcast really came from the island, background bird noises included.

On that same day, by happy coincidence, Munz Northern Airlines gave Chris Robling a courtesy seat on one of its planes flying up the coast. On the way, the plane made several passes over Sledge Island, and Chris — outfitted with a remote transmitter unit — waved to Mark and exchanged greetings with him over the air. One could hear the sound of the plane approaching as Mark talked; then he switched over to Chris inside the plane, who commented on what he saw below.

According to Tom Busch, it was "a thrilling broadcast, another of those ya-hadta-be-there-s!" It lasted two hours, and was the first AM broadcast in history from that island. That it was impressive and captured the imaginations of the listening audience was evident from the generous, positive feedback KNOM received during and after it.

That same July it was again going and coming time. "Railroad Joe" Davis — who was "just passin' through" — stayed to help out with maintenance for a few months. He was to return with his young son, Arlo, in 1984 to do more of the same. Some volunteers stayed on and became part of "that central core of old-timers." Some left KNOM, but stayed on in Nome. Cary Bolling, for example, stayed to work with young people. He was to marry Ann Knobbe a year later in St. Joseph's Church, and go on to direct the media department at Northwest Community College in Nome. Timaree Bierle returned to St. Louis. Radio announcer John Kreilkamp arrived from Gimlet, Idaho; and, shortly after him, nurse Barbara Schlesselmann from California. Jane Schraufnagel, after a year away, returned for another year of nursing. During that summer seminarian J. Albert Levitre did volunteer work at the station. Also helping out that summer was Father Paul Macke, S.J. Father Paul had already spent the previous summer at St. Joseph's.

KNOM and St. Joseph's Staff 1978-1979 (Left to Right) First Row: Holly Nelson, R.N., Denny Gradoville, Pat Knobbe, Bro. Albert Heinrich, F.I.C.; Second Row: Tweet Burik, Dephane Sporrer, R.N., Fr. Harold Greif, S.J., Sue Boyle, Ed Logue; Third Row: Bro. Normand Berger, F.I.C., Trese Ptaszynski, R.N., Fr. Jim Poole, S.J., Jane Schraufnagel, R.N., John Purcell, Joanne Ambrosi; Fourth Row: Eric Gabster, Luella "Mom" Poole, Tom Sofio, Barb Schlesselmann, R.N., John Kreilkamp, Lynn Herich, R.N. *(KNOM Collection)*

Major staff turnover took place a month later. Wrote Father Jim in the August *Static*: "Farewells at KNOM are not exactly easy. Seeing this year's volunteers off was no exception. After a year of generous giving, working and sharing, nurses Ann Knobbe, Ann Diffenbaugh, Zita Schiffelbein, cook Colleen Harrington; radio men Chris Robling, Mark Hoelsken, Chuck Tranfo; maintenance man Pete Fricilone; Dr. Mike McMahon, Father Paul Macke, and seminarian Al Levitre all exchanged farewells with the gang who stayed behind. Our gratitude, prayers, and love follow them; and we hope much happiness lies ahead of them. My mother, Tweet, and I have been doing this for 11 years, and it never gets any easier." Chuck Tranfo, by carefully developing record company contacts, left his mark on KNOM in the many free albums obtained by him in the KNOM record library. Mark Hoelsken, soon after leaving KNOM, joined the Jesuits.

Ann Diffenbaugh went on to marry Iditarod musher Brian Blandford. The two live in a cabin in the wilderness upriver from White Mountain. Early-day KNOMer, Chuck Newberg, too, married — so to speak — the Iditarod, when he married Shirley Nayokpuk, daughter of widely popular Iditarod musher, Herbie Nayokpuk.

The previous March, Colleen Harrington treated the KNOM gang to "a great St. Pat's Day" with a traditional Irish dinner and an Irish jig. In turn she was given an Irish award plaque "for being irrepressibly and irresistibly and irreversibly Irish." From Nome Colleen flew almost directly to Ireland to work there at the Glencree Center For Reconciliation, situated some 12 miles south of Dublin.

Nature abhors a vacuum. So does the KNOM volunteer roster. To fill in the blank spots came radio announcers Ed Logue from Aberdeen, Washington, Eric Gabster from Los Angeles, and Tom Sofio from Inglewood, California. John Purcell came from Seattle to teach C.C.D. classes. And there came nurses: Lynn Herich from Santa Ana, California, and Dephane Sporrer from Portland, Oregon.

They were joined in October by Ann Knobbe's sister, Pat. Pat had visited Ann earlier, and quickly concluded that KNOM was also for her. She came as a dental hygienist support volunteer. Visiting KNOM-Nome can be dangerous. KNOM-Nome fever is highly contagious. Pat caught it, and is now a permanent part of the Nome community — as the wife of Nomeite Bob Walsh.

As the year 1978 wound down, Father Jim made national news. The 18 December issue of *People Weekly* magazine carried an article about him headlined, "WESTERN ALASKA'S HIPPEST DJ IS JIM POOLE, S.J., COMIN' AT YA WITH ROCK'N'ROLL'N'RELIGION." Three pictures of "the cheerful, young-looking Jesuit" illustrate the story. One shows him at the console, another with Eskimo children, a third distributing Holy Communion in St. Joseph's Church.

In response to the article, one reader wrote to the editor: "Thank you so much for the story on Father Poole. From 1971 to 1973 I was a resident of Northeast Cape, and the volunteer voices of KNOM were my only link to what was happening in the outside world. They gave all of us music, laughter, information and friendship on those cold, stormy winter days."

The first volunteer to appear on the KNOM scene in 1979, in January, was maintenance man Denny Gradoville from Cedar Rapids, Iowa. He received a red-carpet welcome, for the station had been without a man in the "build and repair division" for five months. In early May he was joined by Brother Ray Berube — KNOM's third Brother of Christian Instruction — also a maintenance man.

"The following is an actual account," wrote John Kreilkamp, "of the events which took place on a cold, snowy evening in January 1979.

"I was just finishing the 10 P.M. expanded newscast, and was finishing the area weather conditions, when I began smelling something extremely nauseous. Then I noticed smoke filtering up from somewhere around my feet. I quickly jumped up, slammed in a special news interview scheduled to go on next, and tried to find the source of the smoke. All the while the smoke was getting thicker and thicker. Having little success, and being just on the verge of panicking, I phoned Brother Normand Berger. Before the answering party had a chance to say 'hello,' I frantically requested Brother Normand's assistance in locating and extinguishing the source of the fire. The response from the other end of the line was, 'Well, this is Alaska Airlines, what would you like us to do about it?' I quickly slammed the phone down and began redialing. As I waited for the phone to ring at Brother's apartment, I looked over and realized that I had left the microphone on the entire time. Immediately the three phone lines coming into the station lit up, beckoning me to answer. Line one was the Alaska Airlines janitor asking if I needed help. Line two was the fire department inquiring about the story they heard of KNOM being on fire. Line three was a listener asking when we would play that spot again.

"When all the smoke cleared, it turned out that the 'FIRE' turned out to be a plastic relay switch which somehow became stuck and simply melted the surrounding parts, causing a total of $5 in damage."

"In all of my life the most heartbreaking farewell was my departure from Nome," wrote Father Jim in the July 1979 *Static*. After 13 consecutive years in Alaska he was leaving it for a sabbatical year at Berkeley, California, to take refresher courses in theology. Leaving under the same cloud of tearful farewells were John Purcell and Barbara Schlesselmann. They were on their way to toll wedding bells in California — another KNOM couple!

But KNOM was not to be without a Poole for so much as one year. Father Jim's nephew, Mike Ford, had come up in June for a volunteer year as a radio announcer. With him came nurse Anne McCarthy. Anne proved to be not only a compassionate nurse, but also, according to Tom Busch, "one heck of a deejay. She has a great voice and a gentle, easygoing charm that transmits right into the radio. She could make it in the big city." Two Notre Dame Sisters, Julie Marie and Celeste, spent the month of July in Nome teaching the children religion.

Father Paul Macke, S.J., from Chicago, who had already helped out in Nome the previous two summers, came to

Anne McCarthy at the console, 1980. *(Photo by Phil Dunne, courtesy of* The Bering Straights*)*

replace Father Jim during his year of absence. Father Paul was to stay on for three years as a popular pastor and an able radio man.

Departing during the summer of 1979 were Denny Gradoville, "who kept everything together and running, and whose kindness and humor endeared him to all the KNOM gang," and John Kreilkamp, "who did an excellent job deejaying and in production, and who brought a lot of love and caring to the community."

These two were soon followed by nurses Jane Schraufnagel and Trese Ptaszynski, both of whom "did a very loving

KNOM and St. Joseph's Staff 1979-1980. (Left to Right) First Row: Sr. Marion Michalak, Theresa Wiederhold, Bro. Albert Heinrich, F.I.C., Valerie Conger; Second Row: Fr. Paul Macke, S.J., Sue Boyle, Tom Sofio, Betty Powell; Third Row: Tweet Burik, Tim Cochran, Dephane Sporrer, Mike Ford, Sr. Gail Singel, Anne McCarthy, Holly Nelson, Bro. Normand Berger, F.I.C.; Fourth Row: Bro. Ray Berube, F.I.C., Lynn Menke, Eric Gabster, Anita Duenser, Marty Clarke, Kathy Crayon, and Diana Gardenier. *(KNOM Collection)*

job at the hospital and in the KNOM community." One year later Trese became Mrs. Tom Sofio. Yet another KNOM couple!

Joanne Ambrosi, after serving for a year as secretary, then a year as a very dedicated cook, also left at this time. She was noted especially for the quality and quantity of her blueberry pies. Nurse Lynn Herich finished her KNOM year on 30 August, but stayed on in Nome. At this time 20 ex-KNOM volunteers were making their homes in Nome.

In August Ed Logue finished his year as Music Director and "excellent radio announcer," and headed south. He returned the following year for another 6-month tour at KNOM. Al Levitre — "a tremendous help in radio and in the parish" — wound up his second summer in Nome. He headed east to continue his studies preparatory to being

Father Paul Macke saying Mass in the lee of an umiak, Eskimo skinboat, for some King Island Eskimos at their summer camp at Cape Woolley northwest of Nome. *(Photo by Brother Albert Heinrich, F.I.C.)*

ordained a priest in 1980. He was at this time Deacon Levitre, having been ordained to the diaconate that summer, right in Nome, the first Catholic deacon ever to be ordained there. While at KNOM, Al always introduced himself on the air as "Big Al." When people met him on the street and found out that *he* was "Big Al," they did a double take. Father Al is rather short of stature — but a big man, nevertheless. After serving successfully in the Sacred Heart Cathedral parish in Fairbanks, he became pastor of the parishes stretching from Nenana to Cantwell.

Pat Knobbe and Tom Sofio were the last to depart KNOM in 1979, leaving in November. Both left KNOM indebted to them. Tom is gratefully remembered as the man who put much needed order and system into the station's spot programming.

Father Jim receiving the Gabriel Award, 1979, in Los Angeles, from Rev. John Geaney, President of UNDA-USA, the National Professional Association of Broadcasters and Allied Communicators. *(Photo by Pete Andreadis)*

Cheechakos, or newcomers, for the year 1979-80: Diana Gardenier, newsperson, freelance writer, TV producer, and honors graduate from the University of Portland with a degree in communications, from Portland, Oregon; two Adrian Dominican Sisters, Gail Singel and Marion Michalak, to work in the parish and run the Religious Education program; radio announcers Marty Clarke from Chicago and Shawn Hensley and Sue Harding, both from Nome; Anita Duenser, announcer, secretary, then also Religious Education Director, from Chicago; Tim Cochran, announcer from Salmon, Idaho; Theresa Wiederhold, nurse, from Portland, Oregon; Betty Powell, nurse, from Milwaukee; Lynn Menke, nurse, from West Point, Iowa; Val Conger, nurse, from Seattle; and Kathy Crayon, cook, from Escondido, California.

Sue Boyle, who had spent her first year in Nome as C.C.D. teacher, her second as a newsperson, stayed on for a third year, now as News Director. Nurse Holly Nelson also stayed on for a third year, to work with village nursing services. And then there were "the forever faithfuls": Tweet in her 16th year of volunteer work, Brothers Normand Berger and Albert Heinrich both starting their 5th, and Tom Busch his 9th. These tried and true perennials continued to be the anchor people who made the rotating staff concept a viable, a successful one.

While Father Jim was quietly — restlessly — pursuing theological studies at Berkeley — and at the same time entertaining dozens of volunteers, former, and present vacationing ones — the station received the nation's highest Catholic honor for broadcasters, the coveted Gabriel Award. In citing KNOM for the "best station" award, the judges stated, "KNOM functions with a concept of total service to a wide variety of human needs. The creativity utilized to meet the uniqueness of the Alaskan people is outstanding from station operation to the broadcast performance. KNOM makes an outstanding contribution not only in its programming, but also in its concept of volunteerism in its total operation. This is the stuff of which real public service is made. This is broadcasting at its educational, informational, and inspired BEST, imaginatively presented." (Emphasis is theirs.)

Tweet Burik as KNOM Business Manager and Tom Busch as General Manager with the 3½ pound Gabriel statuette awarded KNOM in 1979 in recognition of the station's "outstanding programs which creatively treat human values." *(Photo by Phil Dunne, courtesy of* The Bering Straights)

At a banquet held in the Ambassador Hotel in Los Angeles, on 28 November, the award was accepted — in the name of all who had helped make the KNOM dream a crowned reality — by Father Jim himself. For him and all the KNOM gang, past and present, the 3½-pound statue, and everything it stood for, was a Christmas present come early, a Christmas present without rival. (In 1984 KNOM won *two* Gabriel Awards: one for being the "top radio station in the country," and one for its "Catholic Neighbor" spot series, a set of national inspirational spots KNOM sends to other stations across the country. Add two more Gabriel statuettes to KNOM's growing collection of awards!)

Transmission 20

Back in Nome: 1980

"I'm homesick!" wrote Father Jim in February 1980. His year in exile at Berkeley was obviously getting to be a long one for him. By May he was already in the process of packing for the 13 July return trip to Nome. "Will I ever be glad to be heading home!"

Almost as if to avoid his uncle, but not really, Mike Ford flew south in June, along with Ed Logue. Both went on to jobs in commercial radio.

KNOM spot: *"Can anyone know how I hurt inside? I have lost someone I loved with all my heart, and that heart is broken." "I do," said the Lord. "Come to me and I will comfort you. Your loved one is here beside me, and I will love for you until you come."*

"My trip back to Nome," wrote Father Jim in the July 1980 *Static*, "was sadly interrupted in the Anchorage airport by an emergency call from Fr. Paul Macke in Nome telling me of a plane crash and the death of one of our KNOM volunteers, Diana Gardenier. I was really stunned."

The tragic accident occurred on 12 July, when the Cessna 402 in which she and seven others were traveling, crashed in the fog near Cape Darby, southeast of Golovin, 100 miles east of Nome. The sudden loss of one of its members cast a pall of "overwhelming grief" over the whole KNOM family. Diana — just recently promoted to KNOM News Director — had flown out to do a news story on fishing in Norton Sound villages. All on board were killed instantly.

A broadcast written by Tom Busch and voiced over KNOM by Father Macke the day after the crash read in

part: "Diana possessed a brilliance and a depth of spirit
that has touched each one of us. Knowing Diana, we have
learned a little more about faith, about what it means

Diana Gardenier. *(Photo by Theresa Wiederhold)*

to commit yourself to an ideal, about love and about the spark of divinity within every person, in which Diana believed so much."

Two years earlier she had written about herself: "My existence is significant...I have to use my time, my strength and my talents, my love...some kind of strength is alive in me. It comes from the love I have known, the dreams I have had, the future I can see. If I use this strength to heal one wound, I have fought the whirlpool. If I give one person room to find his own strength, I have made my existence worthwhile."

KNOM and St. Joseph's Staff 1980-1981. (Left to Right) First Row: Theresa Wiederhold, R.N., Joan Cleppe, R.N., Fr. Jim Poole, S.J., Bob Geisinger; Second Row: Fr. Harold Greif, S.J., Harry Owens, Jr., M.D., Tweet Burik, Patrick Kloster, Vicki-Marie Colacicco, R.N., Mary Christine Yanikoski; Third Row: Bruce Jones, Fr. Paul Macke, S.J., Johanna Sheehey, R.N., Tom Kensok, Paula Harr, Anne McCarthy, R.N.; Fourth Row: Tim Cochran, Mary McGoldrick, R.N., Bro. Normand Berger, F.I.C., Mary Jean Sprute, R.N., Bro. Raymond Berube, F.I.C., Anita Duenser, Eric Gabster, Kathy Crayon, Bro. Albert Heinrich, F.I.C. *(KNOM Collection)*

Diana Gardenier, KNOM volunteer, dead at the age of 22. R.I.P.

In August Holly Nelson, Lynn Menke, and Marty Clarke all tearfuly boarded the southbound jet. Four years later, in 1984, the whole KNOM family was again to be saddened, this time by the news that Marty Clarke was killed in an auto accident while on duty as a police officer in Chicago. R.I.P.

By mid-September the following newcomers were on their respective jobs: nurses Joan Cleppe from Richland, Washington; Johanna Sheehey from Burlington, Vermont; Mary McGoldrick from Chicago; Vicki-Marie Colacicco from Chicago, Illinois; cook Paula Harr from Helena, Montana; News Director Bob Geisinger from Chicago; announcers Tom Kensok from Lafayette, California; and Pat Kloster from Yakima, Washington; Music Director and announcer Bruce Jones also from the state of Washington. And from Braintree, Massachusetts, came Features Director Mary Christine "M.C." Yanikoski. M.C. was to put in fully four years of exceptional radio services.

In October Sue Boyle left KNOM — went out in a blaze of Associated Press glory. During her last month at KNOM, she had a grand total of 11 stories accepted by the A.P. — a new record at the time for a KNOMer. Sue made significant contributions to the whole KNOM operation. Among them, she spearheaded the fresh idea of regularly sending KNOM reporters into the villages for news stories.

From KNOM Sue moved on to a reporter-weekend anchor position with KTVF, Channel 11, the number one television station in Fairbanks. After a year in TV, she missed the creativity of radio, as well as the opportunities of covering the people and issues of rural Alaska. She, therefore, took a reporter-producer position with the Alaska Public Radio Network. While with A.P.R.N., she single-handedly brought the public's attention to the Hepatitis B virus epidemic in rural Alaska; and, by doing so, indirectly brought about the funding needed for an immunization program.

Incidentally, Sue has also done her part to strengthen the KNOM-Iditarod bond. She married Iditarod musher Ron Cortte, whom she met while covering the race for KNOM in 1979 and 1980.

Nurse Mary Jean Sprute from Idaho joined the KNOM clan on 15 November. She filled the position vacated by Dephane Sporrer, who left the station but continued on in Nome. (Dephane died in a Willamette River canoeing accident in February 1985. R.I.P.) Val Conger — a member of the Nome women's championship softball team — also left KNOM about this time.

The last addition to the staff in 1980 was Dr. Harry Owens, who arrived from West Africa on 29 December. He came to serve as a volunteer support doctor, working at the hospital and donating his salary to the station. Oldtimers may remember his father, orchestra leader Harry Owens of Hawaiian music fame. The sister of Dr. Owens was the girl in the song "Sweet Leilani."

Transmission 21
Father Jim Goes on
Nationwide TV: 1981

By January 1981 the KNOM community, having grown
to 25, had outgrown its dining table — really just a long
counter lined with bar stools. To provide more elbowroom,
Brother Ray moved the kitchen-dining room wall five feet

KNOM and St. Joseph's Staff 1981-1982. (Left to Right) First Row:
Tweet Burik, Bro. Albert Henrich, F.I.C., Harry Owens, Jr., M.D.,
Peter Neagle; Second Row: Fr. Jim Poole, S.J., Marie Dieringer, Anne
McCarthy, R.N., Ruth Barber, R.N., Fr. Paul Macke, S.J.; Third Row:
M.C. Yanikoski, Anita Duenser, Fr. Harold Greif, S.J., Marilyn Koezuna,
Bill Welborn, Judy Talbot, R.N., Paula Harr; Fourth Row: Tony
Rutledge, Mary Jean Sprute, R.N., Bro. Ray Berube, F.I.C., Polly Yett,
R.N., Bro. Normand Berger, F.I.C., and Tim Cochran. (*KNOM
Collection*)

into Father Jim's office, and lengthened the table to 21 feet seven inches. Quipped Father Jim, "We use semaphore signals to ask for the sugar at table now!"

The first new volunteer on the job for the 1981-82 year was Tony Rutledge from New Jersey. He arrived in April and brought with him several years of commercial radio experience. That same April Father Jim went to St. Louis, at the request of the Sacred Heart Program there, to make six TV shows to be shown nationwide. This was his first effort in television. His televised talks were such a success that two years later he was back there again, to make six more TV shows and 142 radio spots. He had been doing sermons and spots for the Sacred Heart Radio Program since as early as 1947. The Sacred Heart Radio Program has broadcast over a thousand of his sermons and spots.

When the shorefast ice drifts away from Nome, the work of the summer begins in earnest. Fishing skiffs, native skin-boats, nets and floats come off the winter storage racks and are carefully readied for the fishing of the seasonal runs of salmon and herring. Many of the Eskimos move their entire families to summer fish camps, where work lasts as long as the sun hangs in the arctic sky — almost around the clock.

KNOM sees a special responsibility to adapt its programming schedule in such a way as to better serve also the seasonal needs of its primary target audience. Accordingly, in 1981, as in 1980, the station extended its regular 18 hours of broadcasting to 24. For six days a week, during the months of June and July, its frequent, helpful weather, marine, fishing advisories and its friendly companionship went out to those who had to work throughout the twilight night. For its extended service KNOM was rewarded with a "tremendous response" from grateful fishermen and their families.

Shortly before KNOM celebrated its tenth year on the air, Father Jim wrote, "We are approaching a significant trail marker in our radio apostolate. It makes me both justifiably proud and genuinely humble to realize that it was July 14, 1971, that KNOM signed on the air, just ten years ago. Back then there was no assurance of success — just hard work, the support of people like you, and a mountain of good intentions and prayers."

It is interesting to compare the Nome and the KNOM of 1971 with the Nome and the KNOM of 1981. In the

Brother Normand Berger, F.I.C., KNOM's Engineer and Program Director for a decade. (Alaskan Shepherd *Collection*)

Nome of 1971 there was no live television, and only patchy long-distance telephone service. There was no telephone service to the villages. Half of Nome still used honeybuckets and trucked water. Many villages had no electricity, and none had sewer or water systems. During winter storms, Nome would go for as long as five days in a row without jet service. Ten years later, Nome had a full range of satellite channels, and even the villages had two channels of live TV. Most villages also had reliable telephone and electric service, and many even had some kind of sewer and water systems. Nome, by 1981, boasted over 30 high-quality long-distance phone circuits, with crystal clear direct-dial anywhere in the U.S. Nome electricity was, for the most part, reliable. With glide slope equipment at the airport, very few jets were weathered out by storms.

Taking a then-and-now look at the KNOM of 1971 and that of 1981, KNOM inside expert Tom Busch wrote: "KNOM's physical plant, and the station's operation, had grown tremendously. The studios were almost unrecognizable. In 1973 the newsroom and production Studio B each received new consoles. In 1980 Brother Normand installed a 12-channel console in the Control Room, and put the old control console into Studio C, which became a full-fledged recording studio. By 1981 the station had no fewer than seven turntables, ten cartridge tape machines, five reel recorders, three incoming telephone lines, and a full-time audio network. KNOM had two under-the-arm hi-fi UHF transmitters for doing remotes around town, a 40-watt hi-fi VHF transmitter for doing distant remotes, and a handful of other communications gear. It was the natural attendant of KNOM's evolution, since the station had learned how to produce several times more material than before, while broadcasting from 5:55 A.M. to 12:10 A.M. (later to sign on at 5:25 A.M.). KNOM was doing more of everything — features, news, even weather. Still, with all of the differences, KNOM was attempting exactly what it had been trying to do all along. Father Poole's idea of inspiration mixed with a balance of education, news and entertainment had grown more sophisticated with the audience and the times, but it was basically the same. And it was every bit as wildly popular as it had been ten years earlier!"

Concerning TV's coming to Nome and to KNOM, Tom Busch recalled: "Nome TV Cable began operations in Nome in February 1971. Father Poole refused to buy a color television, calling it a waste of money. I was dejected. A week later, he asked me to pick up some freight at Wien. It was a brand new RCA color receiver! It was a wonderful surprise, and we were all delighted."

King Island Eskimo announcer, Marilyn Koezuna, 1977. *(Photo by Tom Busch)*

Benefactors, kept primed by the *Nome Static*, were at this time providing about 40% of the funds needed to keep the station on the air. The rest came from the support positions, the salaries of the volunteer nurses and doctors.

However, it was not only the penny sent and the penny earned, but also the penny saved, that kept KNOM financially viable during its first ten years on the air. All along every effort was made to economize, to cut costs wherever possible. In 1980, for example, Brother Ray Berube started hauling all of KNOM's fuel with a rig he himself had built with a grant from the Catholic Church Extension Society. This saved the station 18 cents a gallon drayage costs. Two years later, to save on heating fuel, he built an arctic entry for the station's back door. With that same Extension Society grant, KNOM bought its own teletype machine, thereby saving a $900 per year leasing cost. The station has saved itself another $900 per year leasing cost by installing its own telephone system. Commenting on KNOM's management of funds, Tom Busch summarized, "There's not much fat around this place, and people who are so generous to give KNOM money can be assured that doggone little is wasted!"

What had KNOM programmed during its first decade of broadcasting? "The numbers alone are staggering," wrote Father Jim. "In 3,650 days of award-winning broadcasting we've kept western Alaskans informed with over 65,000 news broadcasts, half a million weather reports and more than 300,000 area forecasts."

So much for the numbers. "Yet," he wrote on, "the most important factor in KNOM's success has been an element that's impossible to measure, the tireless work of 180 dedicated volunteers. These people have built a solid feeling of good will and friendliness in a land area the size of France. KNOM's cheerful voice and Christian presence have kept the chill of isolation and loneliness and despair away from thousands."

At the time KNOM celebrated its tenth anniversary, it was not only broadcasting news, but had itself become newsworthy, TV newsworthy. In May a crew came from Germany and did a TV documentary on it, and in August station KAKM-TV from Anchorage and "Real to Reel" — the Catholic TV program based in Washington, D.C. — gave KNOM "the old documentary treatment." The station had all along been the subject of magazine and newspaper articles.

During the summer of 1981 Father Paul Macke went Outside to make his annual retreat and to get some rest and recreation. He was spelled off at St. Joseph's by Father William T. "Bill" Burke, S.J., from Chicago. Father Bill, a state of the art fisherman — ties his own flies — hooked many a fish in the Nome area, and got, in turn, hooked

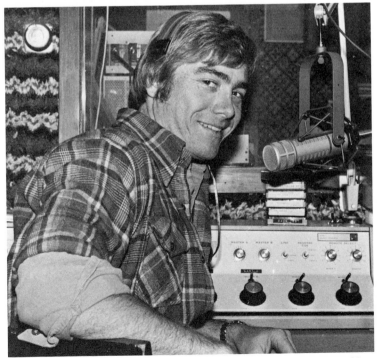

Eric Gabster manning the board, 1981. *(Photo by Tom Busch)*

by Alaska. For some years now he has been the pastor of Delta Junction and dependent missions.

Again, in the summer of 1981, there were two Sisters of Notre Dame, Julie Thorpe and Michela Sheehan, at St. Joseph's. They were up from California to teach a C.C.D. summer school. Jesuit seminarian Pat Hutchings was at the station as an announcer and maintenance man.

Exit, in the spring of 1981, Kathy Crayon, and in July, Music Director Bruce Jones, who with hard work and good

Marie Dieringer deejays from the 12-input console installed in Studio A, 1982. *(Photo by Tom Busch)*

taste did much to further enhance KNOM's music image. Exeunt, in August and September, Bob Geisinger, Tom Kensok, Vicki-Marie Colacicco, Mary McGoldrick, Joan Cleppe, and Johanna Sheehey.

Exit also, after three years at KNOM, Eric Gabster, "top flight morning D.J., become also Production Manager." It was Eric who, along with Tom Kensok and Anne McCarthy, worked out KNOM's acclaimed new program, "Perspectives — A Christian View of News." Of Eric, Tom Busch wrote, "As KNOM's Program Director for three years, he gave KNOM tremendous energy. Eric is a natural leader and fired up the crew during his volunteer years. He is also a generous person, the kind of guy who shovels the steps and takes out the trash when no one's looking." Since his KNOM years, and some advanced studies, Eric has been working for Paulist Communications in Los Angeles, producing news programs which KNOM carries.

Exit, in October, Pat Kloster. And exit, in early December, Mary Jean Sprute, "a very capable nurse and someone who could always brighten our day with her good humor and kindness." Mary Jean subsequently became the bride of former KNOM volunteer Chuck Tranfo. Credit yet one more marriage to matchmaker KNOM!

Soon new volunteers came to fill recently vacated slots. Leading off the 1981-82 rookies were newsman and announcer Bill Welborn from St. Louis, and deejay Peter Neagle, in charge of music, from Branford, Connecticut. Inupiaq Eskimo speaker Marilyn Koezuna of Nome was welcomed back to the staff at this time. From Alhambra, California, came nurse Judy Talbot, and from Portland, Oregon, radio announcer Marie Dieringer, the daughter of one of KNOM's most generous benefactors, Bob Dieringer. Before heading south again, Marie was to put in three years of top-flight KNOM announcing and cooking — along with some support work as a speech therapist in the Nome Public School. Some weeks later nurses Ruth Ann Barber from Stockton, California, and Polly Yett from

Albany, Oregon, arrived to once again round out the KNOM team.

By this time KNOM volunteers had come from 27 different states, plus Canada and the District of Columbia. Washington was first with 23. Alaska had provided 15.

In December 1981 Father Jim was able to report that he had "finally made the team." He was speaking of the Marriage Encounter team, which he "made" by writing 11 acceptable talks and himself making, as it were, three Marriage Encounters — "always a marvelous experience!" Several years and several Marriage Encounters later, he punned, "This is still the most rewarding work I've 'encountered,' an incredibly valuable experience."

Transmission 22

Luella Poole, R.I.P.: 1982

During the earlier part of 1982 three new nurses came to KNOM-Nome to fill in part-time: Mildred Vernosh from Green Bay, Wisconsin; Janet Jezsik from Seattle; and Miriam Sheehey, Johanna's sister. Johanna also came up to help out again for a few months. Jesuit seminarian Joseph "J.P." Reynolds also helped out during the staff-lean months.

At the end of May Brother Albert Heinrich, after rendering six years of varied and much appreciated services — among them meticulous newsgathering and quality work as a photographer — left KNOM to teach high school in Tokyo, Japan. By August sad but grateful goodbyes were in order also for Ruth Barber, for 3-year veterans Anita Duenser and Anne McCarthy, for Tony Rutledge, Paula Harr, Marilyn Koezuna, and Bill Welborn. Another 3-year veteran, Tim Cochran, left in September for Kotzebue, where he became News Director for the radio station KOTZ. When Tim came to KNOM he had no radio experience. But he was a quick learner, and soon he was doing the Morning Show and serving as KNOM's News Director. "These folks," wrote Father Jim, in the August 1982 *Static*, "have given so much and so generously, lovingly; words don't do justice in gratitude."

As usual, replacements had been recruited to carry on where others left off. In August cook Jackie Power from Bisbee, Arizona; nurses Linda Peters from the Bronx, New York, Jane Ritter from Cincinnati, and Debbie Urbanik from Waukegan, Illinois; Youth Minister Maureen Diamond from Ocean City, New Jersey; Religious Education Director Julianne Dickelman from Spokane; and radio personnel Damien and Lynette Berger, brother and sister of

Brother Normand, from Bainbridge, Washington, were welcomed to KNOM. By late 1984 the three Bergers, collectively, had put in a total of 15 years at KNOM. Lynette has been exceptionally successful at feeding news stories to the Associated Press. In 1983 the A.P. accepted more stories from her than from any other radio reporter in Alaska,

KNOM and St. Joseph's Staff 1982-1983. (Left to Right) First Row: Linda Peters, R.N., M. C. Yanikoski, Marie Dieringer; Second Row: Fr. Jim Poole, S.J., Lynette Berger, Peter Neagle, Jackie Power; Third Row: Jane Ritter, R.N., Mo Diamond, Martha Salm, R.N., Randy Romenesko and Terry Romenesko,R.N., Tweet Burik, Harry Owens, Jr., M.D.; Fourth Row: Debbie Urbanik, R.N., Bro. Ray Berube, F.I.C., Bro. Normand Berger, F.I.C., Damien Berger, Juli Dickelman, Herbert Merz, M.D., Christopher Laurion and Christine Laurion, R.N. *(KNOM Collection)*

and in 1984 she was again the A.P.'s top story feeder with a grand total of 42. Runner-up, Tim Cochran — former KNOM News Director, now with KOTZ in Kotzebue — was second with 25. Lynette owed her extraordinary success in part to the word processor KNOM acquired in 1982.

The above were joined later in the year by two married couples: radio man Christopher and nurse Christine Laurion from Lansing, Michigan and Elyria, Ohio, respectively; and radio man Randy and nurse Terry Romenesko from De Pere, Wisconsin. Martha Salm, too, was part of the 1982-83 crew. She had to leave a month early because her father had cancer, but during her stay she was "an absolute pleasure to have in the community — she loved greatly and was greatly loved." Martha is the only volunteer ever to get off the plane again for another round of goodbyes. She later returned to Nome to work there.

In the October 1982 *Static* Father Jim reports the sad, but not unexpected, news: "My mother, who had worked with me in Nome for 13 years and for the past few years had been staying with my sister, had been growing weaker and weaker over the past month. She had been taken to the hospital, and it was clear that the end of her 87-year life was not far off. So we took her home.

"My brother Bob, a doctor, flew in from Hawaii. I flew in from Nome, and all of us were with her every one of the 24 hours a day. She remained clear and conscious until the last day. We had Mass beside her bed every day. Prayers came from family and friends everywhere.

"On October 3rd in the evening, I had been praying with her for about three hours and felt she was close to the end. So I kissed her goodnight and went to bed as my brother took over the watch. At 12:05 A.M. she quietly, peacefully, and without pain went home to God. It was the answer to 30 years of prayers.

"Please join me in thanking God for her love-filled life and the peaceful ending of her life."

Ma Poole — as she was affectionately known to the
KNOM family — cooked all the meals for Father Jim and
his crew during KNOM's early days. Later she served as
the lunch cook. At age 83 she was still "the most active
scrabble player in western Alaska." When Father Jim went
south for his sabbatical year in July 1979, he took her
along Outside, for the last time. The volunteers found it
hard to believe that she would never again be seen sitting
in her customary place of honor near the coffee pot behind
the counter, a place she had occupied for so long. She
spent her last years with her daughter Helen and her family on Fox Island, Washington.

The beautiful, loving mother-son relationship began with
his birth and ended only with her death. Father Jim's
priesthood served but to intensify the relationship. When
he told his mother he planned to become a priest, she

**St. Marys villagers on the bank of the Andreafsky River lunching and
relaxing to the sounds of radio KNOM.** *(Photo by Florence Francis Busch)*

cried for five minutes before she could calm down enough to tell him how happy she was. Of his devotion to his mother Helen wrote, "He always, since he was a small child, always treated her with such love and respect. The 13 years she spent in Alaska with him were the happiest of her life. He was always doing little things for her, and never lost patience."

Luella Poole, dead at the age of 87. R.I.P.

For two summers, and then for three consecutive years, Father Paul Macke did "a great job" as pastor of St. Joseph's. However, in the summer of 1982, while vacationing in Chicago, he contracted a lingering illness that put an end to his years in Alaska. Father Jim again assumed the role of pastor of the Nome parish.

Exit — along with the year 1982 — also Polly Yett, "a marvelous nurse, and a very loving person in the community." Polly left KNOM, but stayed on in Nome where she found another job.

Transmission 23

Senior Citizen: 1983-84

As 1983 dawned, many a teary eye saw the departure of Dr. Harry Owens, "an incredibly nice guy to have in the community." Debbie Urbanik departed in February. About this time Father Gerry Ornowski, M.I.C., arrived to serve for a few months as interim pastor. Father Gerry had helped out in the Nome parish in the summer of 1976. Soon after him arrived new cook Jean Allhoff.

KNOM and St. Joseph's Staff 1983-1984. (Left to Right) First Row: Lori Schwartz, Fr. Jim Poole, S.J., Therese "Tweet" Burik, Mike Dodman; Second Row: Jean Allhoff, Marie Dieringer, Maureen Diamond, M.C. Yanikoski, Lynette Berger, Bro. Normand Berger, F.I.C.; Third Row: Bro. Ray Berube, F.I.C., Dave Fronske, R.N., Chris Gfroerer, Peter McCanna, Juli Dickelman, Damien Berger, Christine Laurion, R.N., and Christopher Laurion. *(KNOM Collection)*

During its 12 years on the air KNOM was required to lower power from 10,000 watts down to 5,000 watts every night. That restriction ended in April, when the station finally received the long awaited federal approval to keep its signal at 10,000 watts day and night. This concession has been very much appreciated by the villages on the outer fringe of KNOM's signal.

That same April KNOM wrote a minor footnote to the history of radio broadcasting when it made the world's first broadcast from a snowblock igloo. The igloo was built on an overnight outing near the summit of Newton Peak, one of the hills ringing Nome, by volunteers Lynette Berger, Peter Neagle, and Jean Allhoff. They were guided by Jim Green, a meteorologist with the national Weather Service stationed in Nome, who first came up with the idea.

The summer of 1983 likewise brought with it the customary changing of the KNOM guard. The nursing staff welcomed marathon runner, backpacker, expert stereoscopic photographer Dave Fronske, RN, from Arizona. Chris Gfroerer came from Ohio to serve as Features Director,

NOME STATIC

TRANSMISSION 214

Alaska Radio Mission
Station KNOM
Box 988, Nome, Alaska 99762
December, 1984

Dear Friend of KNOM,

A very happy and peace filled Christmas season to each and everyone of you! You will all be remembered in a very special way, and so gratefully in all of my Christmas masses and prayers. And I also send greetings for the New Year!

and D.J. Mike Dodman from New York came to work in the News Department, and D.J. Michigan State graduate Peter McCanna came to produce educational spots. Hailing from Washington, D.C., Lori Schwartz arrived to lend a hand as a support volunteer. Mary Hannan came to do some short-term support volunteer work in the Receiving Home, and Ted Mazurak came to do some short-term announcing.

In early 1984 Linda Peters was warmly welcomed back when she returned for another year of service as a support nurse. She was followed by new 1984-85 staff additions: nurses Laurel Erzinger from California, and Catherine Cory from Ohio; radio personalities Dorothy Fister from Pennsylvania, Amy Kerwin from Illinois, Laura Caroompas from New York, Ric Schmidt from Oregon, Mike Jackoboice from Michigan, and George Williams from Anchorage. Mischelle Schirado came from North Dakota to cook for the gang.

The year 1983 saw also a major changing of the clerical guard at St. Joseph's. After having served for 35 years on the missions of northern Alaska — 15 of them in Nome and outlying villages — 83-year-old assistant pastor Father Harold Greif announced that he was leaving the North to go to Spokane to devote his remaining active years to the elderly there. The KNOM and Nome communities needed no less than three farewell parties to show their affection for him and their appreciation for his years of cheerful, generous service in their midst. To compensate for his departure, Father Tom Carlin, the pastor of Little Diomede Island, was reassigned, appointed pastor of the Nome parish.

After living in a 6′×9′ room for 16 years, Tweet was thrilled at the opportunity of being able to live in somewhat more commodious quarters. She moved into the apartment vacated by Father Greif and set about remodeling it. Getting into the spirit of moving, Father Jim — after almost 20 years in a noisy room right off the kitchen-dining area, and shamefully modest in size — decided he, too, needed a bit more space, and especially more quiet. He was now

60 years old, a Senior Citizen, "going down occasionally for a free lunch with the old folks." To celebrate the privileged status that age brought with it — and the 30th anniversary of his ordination to the priesthood — he moved out of the Green House into more spacious quarters in Gleeson Hall. "I am amazed at how much I am enjoying the peace and quiet there," he wrote.

Were age and years catching up with the 3-score disk-jockey priest? Not really. The strong hint of gray in his hair, and the lines in his face — etched there more by his ready smile than by the passing of years — have given him a distinguished look, but he can still pass for a man years younger. The young people always surrounding him, and the dreams he keeps dreaming, continue to keep him young at heart.

He would admit, however, to getting an extra gray hair or two in early 1984 when that other key KNOM man, Tom Busch — who had just completed his year as President of the Alaska Broadcasters Association — flew to Fairbanks to be interviewed by Radio KIAK there, which was prepared

The KNOM gang, with several guests, at dinner, 1984. *(Photo by Louis L. Renner, S.J.)*

to make him a very generous offer, if he would come and work for it. Tom allowed that the offer made him was very tempting. Nevertheless, by that time he had become deeply attached, honor bound to KNOM. To show its appreciation to Tom for his years of unstinting professional service, the Diocese of Fairbanks increased his salary and helped him with land to build a new home for him and his growing family a few blocks from the station.

In 1978 Tom wrote, "KNOM has certainly given me some of the most thrilling and rewarding moments of my life. Also some of the worst headaches and worries." May his continued KNOM connection bring him many more of the former, few of the latter.

Father Jim offering Sunday Mass which is being broadcast over KNOM, 1984. *(Photo by Tom Busch)*

Father Jim was, of course, greatly relieved to know that his General Manager would most likely continue on at the station into the foreseeable future. What he did not know at the time was that he would soon have to be looking for a new Business Manager. In the fall of 1984, the position of secretary to the bishop of the Diocese of Fairbanks opened up. Tweet applied for it, and, after being interviewed, was hired to fill it, effective 1 March 1985. This turn of events hit Father Jim somewhat unexpectedly. Did he worry? Not if he practices what one of his spots preaches.

KNOM spot: *Worry...Worry...Worry...As if we didn't have enough to contend with today, we worry about what's coming up tomorrow. Don't be afraid or worry about tomorrow. God is already there.*

Whatever else Father Jim may be, he is unquestionably a man of deep faith, of unshakable trust in God. The whole radio dream, from the moment first conceived to its full, award-winning fruition, has been seen by him all along as essentially a spiritual enterprise, as his God-given space age apostolate. It is this realization that has enabled him to beg boldly, confidently the Divine assistance he knows to be no less necessary to the station's continued, purposeful existence than is the money begged from benefactors.

KNOM, by now a multimillion dollar venture affecting many, many lives, is heavy stuff, must, therefore, be left in the hands of Him for whose sake and love it was undertaken in the first place. *He* has to see to it that the updates, spots, hotlines, newscasts, songs, homilies, features, advisories continue to go out over the airwaves, that the vital dollars continue to flow in, that competent, dedicated volunteers continue to come to keep it all on the air.

After almost two decades in Nome, and well over a decade on the air, Father Jim has invested a great deal of himself in Nome and in the Alaska Radio Mission. With undiminished enthusiasm he is still committed to both. He is happy in his KNOM-Nome work and more than willing to stick to his microphone ministry — so long as he can carry it out effectively. But, he admits, he is at the same time also ready to let go, to move on to some other priestly work.

The KNOM story and the Father Jim Poole story have here been told as one, for they are, in reality, but one story — so inextricably interwoven are they. However, the story is not over yet. It merely stops here. Stay tuned!